T0366134

Corporate
Resiliency

Corporate Resiliency

MANAGING THE GROWING RISK OF FRAUD AND CORRUPTION

Toby J.F. Bishop
Frank E. Hydoski

WILEY

John Wiley & Sons, Inc.

Published by John Wiley & Sons, Inc., Hoboken, New Jersey.
Published simultaneously in Canada.

For general information on our other products and services, or technical support,
please contact our Customer Care Department within the United States at 800-
762-2974, outside the United States at 317-572-3993 or fax 317-572-4002.

Wiley publishes in a variety of print and electronic formats and by print-on-demand.
Some material included with standard print versions of this book may not be included in
e-books or in print-on-demand. If this book refers to media such as a CD or DVD that is
not included in the version you purchased, you may download this material at http://
booksupport.wiley.com. For more information about Wiley products, visit
www.wiley.com.

Library of Congress Cataloging-in-Publication Data

Bishop, Toby J.
    Corporate resiliency : managing the growing risk of fraud and corruption /
Toby J. Bishop, Frank E. Hydoski.
        p. cm.
    Includes bibliographical references and index.
    ISBN 978-0-470-40517-8 (cloth)
        1. Fraud. 2. Corruption. 3. Risk management. I. Hydoski, Frank E.
II. Title.
    HV6691.B476 2009
    658.4'73—dc22
                                                                    2008052097

10 9 8 7 6 5 4 3 2 1

Contents

Foreword   xi

Preface   xv

Acknowledgments   xix

Introduction   xxi

Part One: Fraud and Corruption Today

Chapter 1: **Can We Eliminate Fraud and Corruption?**   **3**
            Not a pretty picture   3
            Focusing on the larger picture   5
            Potential for catastrophe   6
            Why now?   7
            Resiliency as a corporate goal   10

Chapter 2: **The Growing Risk of Fraud and Corruption**   **12**
            Why should my company be especially
            concerned about fraud and corruption now?   12
            Local problems, global pain   15
            Awareness is crucial   17
            Common sense and observable reality   18
            Tailoring efforts to avert damage   18

Chapter 3: **The Costs of Fraud and Corruption**   **20**
            Higher stakes   20
            Casting a shadow on the future   22

Cost and availability of capital   25
Bad news travels even faster than before   26
Don't expect a slap on the wrist   26

**Part Two: On Becoming Resilient: Strategies
for Avoiding and Minimizing the Impact
of Fraud and Corruption**

Chapter 4: **Building a Resilient Corporation**   **31**
What determines survivability?   31
Reducing vulnerability   32
Traits of a resilient corporation   32
Three key characteristics of resiliency   33
Why resiliency is achievable   33
Learn from the experience of others   34
What are the benefits of fraud and corruption
risk management?   35
Five principles of fraud risk management   37
The first line of defense   39
How can companies use the new guidance?   40
Building resiliency by enhancing fraud and
corruption risk management   40
Corporate resiliency self-assessment tool   42

Chapter 5: **Fraud and Corruption Risk Assessment**   **45**
Behind the facade   45
What is a fraud and corruption risk
assessment?   46
How important is a good fraud and
corruption risk assessment?   47
Implementing fraud and corruption
risk assessments   50
Risk assessment reports: The good, the bad,
and the invisible   58
Four quadrants; four risk management
strategies   61
Questions to ask about your fraud and
corruption risk assessment   64

Chapter 6: **Company-wide Anti-Fraud Controls:**
The Role of the Control Environment
and High-Level Strategies **66**
Creating an anti-fraud control environment 67
What exactly is a *control environment* and
why is it important? 67
Tone at the top 68
The control environment as a bulwark 69
The control environment and governance 70
Put it in writing 71
Setting the tone 71
Internal audit's role 73
Measuring tone at the top 73
Written code of ethics/conduct 74
Why is a code important? 74
Excerpts from Deloitte Code of Ethics and
Professional Conduct 75
How does management create a successful
code of ethics/conduct? 76
Ethics training for all employees—including
management 77
Hotlines, helplines, and whistle-blower
programs 78
The role of human resources—employee
selection and discipline 80
Other general strategies of which fraud risk
management is a component 81
Enterprise risk management 82
Fundamentals of ERM 82
Achieving risk intelligence 83
Fundamentals of GRC 84
Complicated, but worth the effort 85
Integrated versus nonintegrated GRC 85
Survey results show desire for integrated GRC 86
Key attributes of companies with robust
GRC strategies 87
PACI, anti-corruption, and the control
environment 88

Chapter 7: **Preventive Controls: Particular Fraud and**
            Corruption Avoidance Strategies and Tactics   **91**
            Getting down to brass tacks   91
            Confronting fraud and corruption risks   93
            Background checks and enhanced due
            diligence   95
            Automation can be essential   96
            Preventive controls and three broad
            categories of risk   96
            Monitoring and evaluating preventive controls   100
            Continuous controls monitoring   102
            Correcting deficiencies   103
            The roles of ERM and GRC   104

Chapter 8: **Detective Controls and Transaction Monitoring** **105**
            The importance of monitoring and detection   105
            Monitoring and detection tactics   107
            Whistle-blower hotlines   107
            Risk-based internal audits as a fraud
            detection tactic   110
            Manual monitoring   112
            Technology-based detection tactics   112
            Examples of fraud detection using
            data interrogation techniques   114
            Continuous fraud monitoring   117
            Is CFM for everyone?   119
            The importance of lookbacks as a
            control check   120
            Questions to ask about monitoring
            and detection   121

Chapter 9: **Preparing for Fraud and Corruption**
            Investigations and Remediation   **122**
            Be prepared   122
            An ounce of planning . . .   124
            What to do when regulators come knocking . . .   125
            Evaluating the allegation   126
            Assembling the right investigation team   127
            When to call for help   128
            Establishing investigation protocols up front   129

Collecting and preserving crucial data   130
Newer challenges, newer technologies   131
Communication—enough but not too much   133
The benefits of a case management system   133
Remediation—getting more value from
investigations   134

Chapter 10: **The Players' Roles (Including Yours)**   **136**
New rules, new responsibilities   136
The value of a cross-functional committee   146
The role of the compliance officer   147
Fraud and corruption risk management is
everyone's business   148

Conclusion: **What the Future May Hold**   **151**
Good fraud and corruption risk
assessment is crucial   153
Embracing new roles and responsibilities   154
Measuring performance   155
We won't predict the future, but . . .   155
Take your first steps now   156

Afterword   157

Appendix: Examples of Fraud Risk Factors   161

Recommended Reading   169

References   173

Disclosure   189

About the Authors   191

Index   193

Foreword

This book is for those of you who participate in corporate governance and management, and are grappling with your organization's need to manage fraud and corruption risk in your operations and strategic planning. It is for those of you who do not have the time, and whose companies do not have the resources, to spend on investigating and defending major fraud or corruption incidents in your organization.

If you hold, or have held, any senior role in corporate management or governance, you may already understand that you are doing so at a time when scrutiny of your role and the expectation that your organization will operate transparently and ethically have never been higher. The world's economy and markets, steadily shrinking, have never provided so little in the way of resources or revenue to do so. And these circumstances have only increased political and public intolerance of corporate misfeasance and mismanagement, especially in the areas of fraud and corruption.

Add to this a revolution in global enforcement and regulation, which now follows commerce across borders with lightning speed. Ten years ago, it would have taken months for local or national prosecutors to obtain the attention, much less the assistance, of colleagues on another continent. But in the beginning of this century the war on terrorism required instant international communication among law enforcement agencies, and corporate investigations and prosecutions rapidly adopted these practices. By 2006, when the investigation of the United Nations Oil-for-Food Programme had been completed, prosecutors and regulators from dozens of countries were regularly meeting to sort out dozens of corruption cases.

The time needed to investigate a single cross-border matter has now shrunk from years to weeks. Simultaneous raids of corporate offices in multiple countries are no longer unusual events. Multiple fines and sanctions, levied as on a single company, regularly exceed hundreds of millions of dollars and can wipe out a year's worth of profits with the swipe of a pen.

You may have already witnessed first hand the cost of the investigation and defense of a fraud or corruption incident in your organization. The costs often rival the fines your organization hoped to avoid. Some employees, officers, or board members may have been held personally responsible. And you and your colleagues may have already realized that something far less costly could have been done to avoid this, if the organization had been sensitive to the risks that your company faced.

In this book, Toby Bishop and Frank Hydoski distill for senior managers and board members their experience in the most effective ways in which businesses can build and develop strong fraud and corruption risk management strategies. The authors, who have conducted investigations and evaluations of hundreds of organizations, are recognized as leading authorities in fraud risk management and innovators in forensic accounting and risk management practices. Toby co-authored the Institute of Internal Auditors/ AICPA/ACFE 2008 paper, *Managing the Business Risk of Fraud*. Frank has led two of the largest international investigations of fraud and corruption, the investigations of the Holocaust-era accounts held by Swiss banks and of the United Nations Oil-for-Food Programme. He was instrumental in formulating recommendations on UN operations following the latter.

In keeping with their reputations, the authors of *Corporate Resiliency* provide a new approach borne from their extensive insight and common sense. The traditional, reactive view of corporate fraud and corruption risk management is often that of the media, prosecutors, regulators, and legislators who arrived at the scene of the crimes, or sometime afterword. To be useful, these stories need to be rewound to find the circumstances that led up to them, and then fast-forwarded to test the processes a company put in place after the fact to see if the processes actually reduce the risk of these incidents occurring. Bishop and Hydoski employ a deliberate review of this cycle to demonstrate the value of developing corporate resiliency through the ability of a corporation to prevent, detect, investigate, and remediate these risks, and to test and adjust risk management systems to account for the constantly changing signature of these risks. What the authors demonstrate is that this is not guesswork, but a strategy that can be successfully applied by you and your company and that can reap real bottom-line benefits for the organization.

Corporate Resiliency offers managers and directors a holistic approach to the management of fraud and corruption risk that speaks to the same measures of productivity and profitability used in more conventional business processes. It walks the reader through the relationships among the board of directors, the audit committee, senior management and staff in the process of fraud risk management, with a clear eye toward the intent and direction of fast-changing legislation and regulatory guidance.

It makes clear the value of the continuous development of a comprehensive, self-evaluating fraud and corruption risk management program that operates with and through existing business processes and that is championed by the board and management. It outlines the essential role of the internal audit function in the regular assessment of compliance programs, the risk of management override of corporate controls, and the monitoring of fraud and corruption risk programs.

It points out, tellingly, that courts and government regulators faced with instances of corruption and fraud will not simply focus on whether a company has a process to manage that risk, but on the effectiveness of the process and on how well tended it is by the corporation's board, management, and risk professionals.

Continuous, self-evaluative risk management processes are not new, but *Corporate Resiliency* is one of the few works that explains the essentials of this risk management structure, and in doing so makes it obvious that today's directors and managers ignore the management of fraud and corruption risks at their own peril.

Mark G. Califano
Head of Litigation
GE Capital Finance

Preface

A recent article in the *Wall Street Journal* carried the headline, "U.S., Other Nations Step Up Bribery Battle." Only a few weeks earlier, an article titled "Guilty Plea to Bribery Sets Legal Landmark" ran in the *Financial Times*. About a year before those articles were published, CFO.com ran an article with the title, "Count' Em: 63 CFOs Convicted in Past Five Years."

These are only three data points among thousands demonstrating the global trend toward stricter enforcement of anti-fraud and anti-corruption laws. Investigations are increasing, prosecutors are getting tougher, fines are becoming heavier, settlements more expensive, and violators are going to jail with far greater frequency than in the past.

Tolerance of bribery as an accepted business practice is diminishing rapidly as more countries acknowledge the tremendous downside risks of corruption and the fraud that almost always accompanies it.

The Sarbanes-Oxley Act ("Sarbanes-Oxley"), the Patriot Act, and the U.S. Foreign Corrupt Practices Act have armed U.S. prosecutors with a formidable arsenal of legal weapons. New support from the global community has boosted U.S. efforts, greatly extending the power and reach of numerous governmental agencies tasked with combating fraud and corruption.

At the same time, there are no indications that attempts to perpetrate acts of fraud and corruption are abating. If anything, the creativity and willfulness of people involved in fraud and corruption seems inexhaustible. "What every senior executive needs to know about anti-fraud strategy is that you're never going to be able to plug all the holes in your organization," says Elizabeth Truelove McDermott, director of internal audit at DeVry Inc. "There's always going to be somebody that finds a hole that no one knew was there."

Like time and tide, fraud and corruption are apparently perpetual phenomena. That doesn't mean that we excuse them or accept them. It means that we need to develop better systems and strategies for dealing with them. It means that we need to acknowledge that the piecemeal, shotgun approaches often relied on in the past to reduce fraud and corruption are unlikely to be effective in today's environment.

The revelation in December 2008 of an alleged $50 billion fraud at Bernard Madoff Investment Securities seems strong evidence of that, especially since the alleged fraud was reportedly simply a classic Ponzi scheme and yet it apparently deceived some substantial investors.

Some readers, no doubt, will argue that programs and techniques for combating fraud and corruption have advanced markedly since the passage of Sarbanes-Oxley in 2002. To some extent, they are correct.

For example, corporate governance is no longer a phrase bandied about largely by academics. New technologies make it possible to automate some anti-fraud controls on a truly global scale. Cross-functional, enterprise-wide approaches to managing fraud risks have become more common across the corporate landscape. It is increasingly rare to find a large company that does not have a written code of ethics and conduct.

Despite these real gains—or perhaps because of them—we believe that many organizations may have developed a false sense of security. They may have been lulled into believing that by "checking the boxes," they have somehow eliminated or greatly reduced the chances that fraud or corruption will happen to them.

For example, Sarbanes-Oxley requires publicly held companies to have a confidential reporting mechanism, such as a whistleblower hotline. It is a key control, especially for dealing with the management override of controls that is a common feature in many of the largest corporate frauds. Yet at some companies, the hotline is underused compared with industry averages. Does that mean there is no fraud or corruption at those companies?

Well, it can mean that. Or it can mean that employees are not aware of the hotline, or that for a variety of cultural reasons, they are afraid to use it. Or maybe the hotline is not getting any calls because it is available only from 9 A.M. to 5 P.M. and employees do not want to be overheard calling from their cubicle. Or perhaps the hotline is only operated in English, creating obstacles for employees who speak other languages.

"When you peel back the layers of the onion, you find all kinds of reasons why people are not using the whistle-blower hotline," notes our colleague Donna Epps. "Just because you have a hotline set up does not mean it is working effectively."

The illusion of security may be amplified by a general lack of transparency and the absence of strong, universal standards that might enable organizations to accurately measure the effectiveness of their anti-fraud efforts. As Donna puts it, "There really has not been a detailed framework for comparing anti-fraud programs, and as a result, there has been a real diversity of practice—not all of it good."

The wide range of practices, the absence of explicit standards, the dizzying array of fraud and corruption schemes, in addition to the speed with which new schemes arise make it tempting for some organizations to view compliance as an acceptable end-point. After all, they might reason, if it is impossible to eradicate fraud and corruption entirely, why take the trouble to go beyond the required minimums?

In some instances, no doubt, achieving a state of regulatory compliance might be considered to be an adequate defense against many types of fraud and corruption risks. But for the vast majority of organizations, merely complying with the existing regulations will not be enough to mitigate the risks posed by fraud and corruption.

If you are really serious about effectively managing the risks of fraud and corruption, we recommend that you take a business approach and focus more on performance and effectiveness rather than just compliance. You will also need a better strategy.

Under the umbrella of this better strategy, you would identify your key fraud and corruption risks and implement processes to manage each of those key risks. Different risks may be best dealt with using different tactics, but your approach would be coordinated, efficient, and transparent to those charged with governance. It would involve many people and become a part of everyone's responsibility. It would require new kinds of thinking, along with more effective involvement of senior management.

As we will show in this book, the downside risks of fraud and corruption more than justify the efforts required to develop a workable fraud risk management strategy. We will build a case for managing fraud and corruption risks on a strategic level. We will show you how fraud and corruption have become too expensive and too dangerous to manage the old way.

When management books describe the characteristics of successful companies, they tend to use words and phrases such as *innovative, customer-centric, first-to-market, disruptive, world-class,* and ultracompetitive. We would like to add a word to that list. The word is *resilient*.

We believe that in the 21st century global economy, organizations need to be more than smart, sharp, and fast. They also need to be resilient in regard to the risks of fraud and corruption. Companies can achieve resiliency by identifying the risks they face and developing strategies for managing those risks effectively.

We honestly do not think that you can count on being successful for very long without being resilient. That is the basic premise of this book.

The views expressed in this publication are solely those of the authors and not necessarily those of Deloitte Financial Advisory Services LLP. We hope you will nevertheless find useful the observations and insights we offer. As used in this book, "we," "our" and "us" refer to the authors. We would be happy to receive your feedback and suggestions for enhancements to this book. We can be contacted through the Deloitte Forensic Center at www.deloitte.com/forensiccenter.

— Toby J.F. Bishop and Frank E. Hydoski

Acknowledgments

Although this book reflects our years of collective experience in forensic accounting and forensic technology, we could not have written it without tapping into the knowledge, insight, and wisdom of many colleagues, clients, and friends. To them we are indebted deeply. We thank them sincerely for their time, their energy, their support, and their patience.

We are especially thankful for the support and guidance provided to us by Frank Piantidosi, Chief Executive Officer, Deloitte North American Financial Advisory LLC.

Over the course of researching and writing this book, we benefited greatly from the assistance of many wonderful clients and friends, including those quoted in this book: Martin Biegelman, Nancy Zucker Boswell, Dr. Olivier Brasseur, Mark Califano, Bill Coleman, Barry Goldsmith, Hugh Hooker, Gavin Ingram, Christian Kammer, Paul Lucas, Elizabeth Truelove McDermott, Mike Novosel, Ed Rosenberg, Duleep Thomas, Paul Volcker, and Joseph Wells.

As Isaac Newton famously remarked, "If I have seen further it is by standing on the shoulders of Giants." With that thought in mind, we thank all of our colleagues at Deloitte who have been key to helping us shape and write this book, particularly Mohammed Ahmed, who provided insightful assistance to us throughout. We would not have been able to write *Corporate Resiliency* without the participation and cooperation of all our colleagues.

We owe special thanks to our Deloitte Forensic Center colleagues Kimberley Davis, Beth de Turo, Jo Ann Hernandez, Reena Panchal, Shaunna Randolph, Edward vanEckert, and Christopher Wharton. Their unflagging efforts were critical to the successful completion of the project.

We also specially thank Mike Barlow, who helped guide the writing process and who shared his editorial expertise with us throughout the endeavor.

All writers, of course, need many additional pairs of eyes. We were especially fortunate to work with Tim Burgard and Sheck Cho, our editors at John Wiley & Sons, who had faith in the value of our project.

We also thank our spouses, who put up with the anxieties and difficulties projects like this always entail. We hope the result is worth their efforts as well as the efforts of our colleagues noted above.

Introduction

T his book is written expressly for executives and others responsible for managing fraud and corruption risks in corporations. It is a concise overview of both the challenges posed by fraud and corruption to modern corporations in a global economy and the techniques for addressing them.

In addition to highlighting categories of fraud and corruption risks, we present a brief series of focused operational strategies that can be deployed to manage these risks and reduce the harmful consequences of fraud and corruption when they occur.

It would be naive to assume that any set of strategies, no matter how rigorous or complex, could totally eliminate fraud and corruption. It would be equally foolhardy, and potentially disastrous, to adopt a fatalistic attitude.

Although we believe that fraud and corruption cannot be fully eradicated, we know that some opportunities for committing them can be shut down. We also believe that many companies can do a better job of identifying fraud risks generally and managing them. In addition to preventing some occurrences of fraud, companies can minimize the damaging effects of fraudulent events and curtail their impact on the corporation.

This book uses the concept of resiliency to provide a practical framework for achieving these objectives. Resiliency is the quality of returning to form following stress. With respect to fraud and corruption, we believe resiliency means a combination of avoiding problems through appropriate planning and risk management, reducing vulnerabilities such as by using early warning systems, and limiting impact by establishing processes that help effect a quick return to business. We suggest that the appropriate goal of companies is the adoption of policies and processes that lead to resiliency in regard to the risks of fraud and corruption.

Talk is cheap, fraud is not

When we think of corporate fraud, we tend to think of the cases that are currently making headlines and those that arose within the past several years. It is likely that the ones you have heard about are the tip of the iceberg. Data analyzed by government agencies such as the U.S. Securities and Exchange Commission (SEC) and professional organizations such as the Association of Certified Fraud Examiners (ACFE) reveals that fraud drains billions of dollars from the economy each year.

In addition to reducing profits, fraud can lead to a host of other negative consequences, including losses of reputation, customer support, access to capital, brand power, market position, competitive advantage, momentum, innovation, and talent. The same, of course, can be said about corruption.

In today's highly leveraged global economy, major fraud or corruption can set off a chain reaction resulting in serious corporate harm or failure.

Economy down; fraud up?

Since the "Crash of 2008" led to economic conditions softening dramatically around the globe, fraud risks for businesses appear to be on the rise. A slowing economy may increase pressure on corporate executives to meet performance goals set in rosier times, or to demonstrate that the current executive team should be retained by shareholders. Individual managers may feel a much greater risk of job loss than usual, potentially making them eager to avoid having to report a performance shortfall in their operating unit.

At the same time, employees may be under greater personal financial pressure, whether due to potential foreclosure on their home, the loss of a spouse's income due to layoffs, or other impacts of the economic downturn.

Add in the possible weakening of internal controls that can inadvertently be caused by corporate layoffs and you have a potent recipe for a potential increase in fraud.

Gavin Ingram, corporate counsel Asia for BlueScope Steel, the leading steel company in Australia and New Zealand, recognizes that the risks of business conduct issues may increase during downturns in the economic cycle. He says, "Tough times are when the organization becomes more susceptible to business conduct issues.

This is probably the time we're at the highest risk of these sorts of issues happening. At such a time it is necessary to remind employees of the importance and expectation around business conduct compliance. People within the company must take an even more active role in reinforcing the message around business conduct."

We concur. While a simple inverse relationship between economic activity and fraud would be an oversimplification, our experience suggests that we may have entered a new cycle of revelations of fraud that could last for several years.

In early 2008, the UK's Financial Services Authority published its annual Financial Risk Outlook in which it stated that, "Tighter economic conditions could increase the incidence or discovery of some types of financial crime or lead to firms' resources being diverted away from tackling financial crime." With the benefit of hindsight, that looks like prescient guidance.

What you don't know *can* hurt you

Managing the risk of fraud and corruption requires an ongoing commitment to acquiring fresh knowledge and putting it to work. Quite often this fresh knowledge must be obtained from outside your company. Organized criminal groups constantly evolve new fraud schemes to part companies from their money. Customer and vendor frauds develop new twists, taking advantage of new technologies.

Entering new markets creates new business opportunities, but also new risks that may be outside your previous experience. You will need a proactive strategy for staying abreast of new fraud risks as they emerge, and a process for sharing critical knowledge across the company as it becomes available.

Ignorance, whether accidental or willful, will not help your company manage the risks of fraud and corruption.

Risk comes at you faster every day

The speed at which fraud risks evolve is accelerating and will likely continue to do so. All we can offer in terms of solace is advice to get used to it and to embrace techniques, which we will describe in this book, to reduce risk and minimize impact.

Thanks to the rapid emergence of global markets, the rise of high-speed digital information technologies, and the ubiquity of the Internet, fraud can now evolve, mutate, and spread with mind-numbing speed. Companies need to be able to adapt with similar speed. Yesterday's processes may not be agile enough.

Manage different categories of risk differently

Despite their sheer numbers, fraud schemes can be divided into a handful of risk categories based on the degree of threat they represent to your company. Each category can be managed effectively with different strategies, helping companies focus their anti-fraud and anti-corruption resources to mitigate risk efficiently. Simple frameworks can help manage fraud risks across companies, large or small.

This is the key takeaway: Fraud and corruption risks can be better managed, and the practical frameworks for managing fraud risks effectively already exist.

"Mind the gap"

Even the best and most practical strategies for managing fraud risks will not be effective if they are not deployed properly across the company.

Our work has identified a *gap* in important areas of fraud risk management at many companies. The upside of this gap is that many of these companies have significant opportunities for greatly improving their fraud risk management processes—and achieving advantages over their competitors.

The gap can be a benefit for nimble companies that recognize their fraud risks and develop strategies to deal with them effectively. By the same token, the gap can be a competitive disadvantage for companies that either ignore their fraud risks or fail to deploy rational fraud risk management programs.

Technology is a tool—use it (wisely)

As suggested above, the danger of fraud has been amplified by the ability of fraudsters to leverage modern technologies such as computers and the Internet.

Conversely, the ability of companies to monitor business processes for potential fraud and to respond quickly when fraud events occur has been greatly enhanced by the availability of technologies such as anti-money laundering (AML) software, advanced analytics, and enterprise financial management systems.

Technologies such as these do more than just level the playing field in the fight against fraud—they help companies enforce higher standards of compliance, transparency, and efficiency.

While it would be unwise to rely solely on technology to manage fraud risks, it is fair to say that technology will play a crucial role in your company's anti-fraud efforts. As an executive, it's important to understand both the potential benefits of advanced technology, and its inherent limitations.

It is also reasonable to suggest that the critical role of information technology argues in favor of a closer relationship between the chief information officer and the company officers responsible for managing fraud and corruption risks.

Who's on first?

Whose job is it to prevent fraud and corruption? Ask that question and you might often hear, "Not me," or "Internal Audit does that."

But managing these risks effectively requires involvement and commitment from employees, managers, and executives in every part of the company. They are the eyes and ears of the company and are often in the best position to identify potential issues and take action to prevent or quickly put a halt to fraud and corruption. They need to be educated and supported to do this effectively.

In fact, we will argue that managing fraud and corruption risks also requires a level of commitment from partners and allies outside of your company.

As an executive, it is your responsibility to encourage a corporate culture that deals honestly and effectively with fraud risks. In addition to "walking the talk," you are also expected to designate the appropriate resources, both capital and human, to ensure that fraud risk management strategies are developed, implemented, and accepted across the company.

Designating the right people for key positions and holding them accountable for managing fraud and corruption risks effectively are crucial parts of your role as a top executive. What gets measured gets done, so effective accountability requires good measurement processes, too.

Our goal in writing this book is to support your efforts to help your company achieve a state of resiliency in the face of fraud and corruption, helping it to survive and succeed in the increasingly risky conditions of the 21st century.

Basic reasons for implementing fraud and corruption risk management programs and controls

Corporate benefits

- Greater chance of survival
- Protect shareholder value
- Greater profitability through loss reduction
- Reduced risk of criminal prosecution
- Enhanced organizational reputation
- Reduce management distractions
- Employee recruitment and retention

Individual benefits

- Reduced risk of criminal prosecution
- Enhanced personal reputation
- Greater career opportunity
- More attractive workplace
- Reduced risk of job loss

Harmful impacts of fraud and corruption

- Potential criminal prosecution or reputations destroyed for people involved
- Direct financial impact (e.g., fraud losses, cost of investigations, civil lawsuits)
- Indirect costs (e.g., loss of customers, management distraction, loss of business opportunities, diminished brand value)
- Negative public relations (e.g., reputation, brand image)
- Decline in share price
- Decrease in corporate governance ratings
- Impact on recruitment and retention of talented employees

PART

I

FRAUD AND CORRUPTION TODAY

Can We Eliminate Fraud and Corruption?

Key points:

- ➤ Fraud itself cannot be eradicated, but fraud and corruption risks can be managed like other business risks.
- ➤ Fraud and corruption risk management strategies can help companies avoid some frauds and help them reduce the impact of frauds that occur.
- ➤ Resilient corporations focus more on strategies, not tactics, for managing fraud and corruption risks intelligently.
- ➤ In today's more brittle economy, fraud and corruption can more easily set off a chain of events resulting in significant loss for the companies affected.

Not a pretty picture

It is quite likely that fraud has existed in one form or another since the earliest days of organized societies. Despite the fact that it is illegal in most countries, despite the vigorous enforcement of anti-fraud laws in many countries, despite corporate self-policing, and despite significant attempts in many companies to create more ethical cultures, fraud continues to be an inevitable and unpleasant component of modern life.

Duleep Thomas, former senior vice president and general auditor at Wyndham Worldwide Corporation, describes this harsh reality this way, "Senior management needs to acknowledge that fraud can occur anywhere, at any time, and at any company. It is not okay to say, 'We operate in an environment of trust.' Once you accept this reality, then you need to understand where fraud could be perpetrated—both internally and externally—with respect to the business."

In general, fraud means taking financial advantage of another party through deception. Frauds affecting companies, the subject of this book, take a variety of forms. They can be threats from outside and carried out by members of the public. For example, they can be false claims made to a medical insurer, in which claims are made for injuries or ailments that the claimant does not suffer. They can also be threats from within and carried out by employees. An example of this would be procurement or vendor fraud, in which an employee sets up a false vendor in the company's accounts payable, then submits bills for goods or services, and collects payments in an account controlled by the employee.

One of the most dangerous form of fraud for a company occurs when the fraud is committed in the name of the company. Examples are misleading claims about products, offering returns on investment that can never be realized, or false financial statements designed to mislead analysts and investors.

Fraud prevention remains an imperfect art for most companies, with less than perfect results. Fraud in the corporate world, therefore, seems an inevitable fact. This is the result of several factors. First, we need to accept the reality that some people will resort to deception if they see an opening. Second, and building on this psychological fact, we need to recognize the lag in time between when schemes are invented and applied, and when they are detected and placed into the knowledge base that fraud prevention techniques rest on.

Third, there is also the difference between what is generally known about fraud schemes and prevention techniques, on the one hand, and what is known and practiced by a particular company, on the other. To stop the fraud schemes that are generally known requires that companies learn about them, evaluate the risks they pose, and diligently apply lessons learned.

The creativity of those who commit fraud seems inexhaustible. As a result, fraud itself can seem more like a disease than a simple criminal phenomenon. Its tendency to mutate suggests a cancer-like quality. Its ability to mask or change its appearance suggests some sort of predatory virus.

However, as we learn about fraud schemes and their character-istics, we *can* act to prevent them. A significant part of this book is devoted to strategies for applying knowledge about fraud in order to try to prevent it, and certainly to detect and limit the effects of schemes.

"It is unlikely that we will ever be able to eliminate fraud and corruption completely. In some societies, it is systemic," says our col-league Mary Jane Schirber. "The more we trade globally, the more likely we are to conduct business in countries with different social norms. It is natural for different cultures to have different customs, and it is important for us to remember that many of the rules we are accustomed to following are not followed everywhere."

That said, it is also important to remember that fraud often accompanies corruption (usually as a way of compensating for the money paid out as bribes) and that the true victims of fraud and corruption are usually innocent people.

"Instead of receiving fair value in a business transaction or exchange of goods, they are getting less than fair value in the form of shoddy products, inferior services, or substandard food," says Schirber. "So they are being hurt by a system they do not have the power to change."

Focusing on the larger picture

It is worth noting that there are accelerating factors involved in the prevalence of fraud and corruption in the contemporary world. These include changing social norms, the democratization of finance, and the unintended consequences of two decades, worth of market dereg-ulation. It also seems clear that our collective ability to fight fraud, on a company-by-company basis, has been hampered by a lack of appreci-ation for what can happen when vigilance is inconsistent and urgency is lacking.

As a society, we have tended to focus more on anti-fraud tac-tics than on anti-fraud strategies. In this book, we will argue that the companies that are successful in avoiding the consequences of fraud employ strategies that allow them to be resilient. Such compa-nies focus on developing practical strategies, workable frameworks and robust processes for preventing fraud, detecting fraud when it occurs, and responding appropriately to minimize the impact of fraud after it has occurred.

During one of our many conversations while writing this book, we realized that the fight against fraud and corruption is in many ways similar to the quest for good health. Our dieting, exercising, and annual physicals won't prevent us from dying one day—but they will help us to live longer, healthier, and more fulfilling lives.

Just because a company has a great risk management program in place does not guarantee that it will never experience an incident of fraud or corruption—but it does mean that when it occurs, the company is likely to recover more quickly and suffer less damage than a company that has been getting by with minimum efforts.

We suggested that fraud and corruption share some similarities with disease. Some diseases we learn to cure; some we learn to treat. We have not yet discovered a "cure" for fraud and corruption, but we can do a lot to make companies resilient and to mitigate their effects.

Potential for catastrophe

Make no mistake—fraud is a problem that drains hundreds of billions of dollars from the economy each year. In addition to directly reducing corporate profits, fraud can lead to a host of other negative consequences down the road. This includes losses of brand power, reputation, market position, competitive advantage, momentum, innovation, revenue, and equity.

In today's highly leveraged global economy, any one of those losses can set off a chain reaction leading to catastrophic results for a company.

Worse, fraud and corruption have a corrosive and damaging effect on a key driver of progress—the competitive spirit. Fraud dampens the human urge to compete because it creates uneven playing fields and rewards behaviors that are fundamentally uncompetitive.

It is no exaggeration to say that the qualities associated with fraud—secrecy, deception and the destruction of value—are the polar opposites of the qualities we now consider essential for success in today's markets—transparency, candor, and the creation of value.

Why now?

Ongoing legal and regulatory requirements, board pressure, and increased media coverage have created a new sense of urgency and have raised legitimate questions about whether companies are prepared to deal effectively with the complexities of fraud in a global economy.

For example, despite the fact that the Foreign Corrupt Practices Act (FCPA) has been around for years, it has only recently become an issue for many companies. Prosecutions of FCPA violations have increased rapidly over the past several years, due to increased focus by U.S. and other authorities on anti-corruption. Several years ago, bribery violations would not have been on the horizon as major risk concerns. Today, for companies dealing with officials in other countries, they can be paramount, thanks to recent international fines and penalties as high as $1.6 billion for a single company.

The unnerving speed at which new fraud risks appear and grow seems to argue for a new kind of corporate agility based on risk management processes supported by advanced analytical technologies. These newer technologies enable companies to develop forward-looking capabilities for anticipating and responding quickly to new risks as they emerge.

Ed Rosenberg, vice president, corporate security for financial institution CIBC, says, "The nature of the threat has expanded. The level of complexity or sophistication of the threat has changed. You need to be responsive to these changes and recognize that sometimes your controls need to be enhanced, need to be altered. The ability to use information from monitoring systems to predict patterns or to identify something that has gone wrong has been very valuable."

What we hope to show in this book is that part of the answer to "Why now?" lies in the knowledge and tools that are currently available to blunt the risk of fraud. In other words, aligning with the sense of urgency is an expanding body of knowledge, techniques, and strategies that can help companies today.

At the head of the list of such techniques and strategies are ways to tackle the diversity of fraud, as well as its changing face, and visualize the relationship between the likelihood of a fraud event in a particular company and its impact on the company. Equally important, there is today a sound set of strategies for deflecting the threats identified and, after the fact, dealing with those not yet understood.

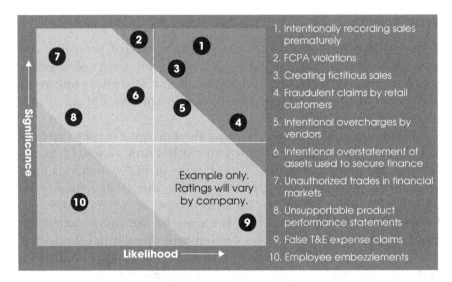

Figure 1.1   Sample "Heat Map"

The start of any fraud and corruption risk management strategy is an assessment of the risks facing a company. The details are commonly assembled in a spreadsheet or database, which can be great for control purposes but may not be easy for senior executives or directors to interpret quickly. A "heat map," which illustrates cold to hot risk scenarios, can be a great way to communicate the key results. A sample heat map of fraud and corruption risks shows the likelihood of specific risks and the potential significance of each item's impact, as shown in Figure 1.1.

This sample "heat map" depicts the hypothetical results of a fraud risk assessment for one company with ten risks identified. The map is simplified since in reality there would often be many more risks identified that would be grouped together, or not considered significant and omitted entirely. Fraud and corruption risks, and the resulting heat map, would vary by industry and by company based on the entity's facts and circumstances. Your company's fraud and corruption risk heat map might look quite different.

If we placed heat maps representing different time periods over the course of two or three years next to each other, we would see the fraud risks evolving over time. Think for example, about stock option administration. A chart looking ahead to the year 2006 could likely be very different from the chart looking ahead to

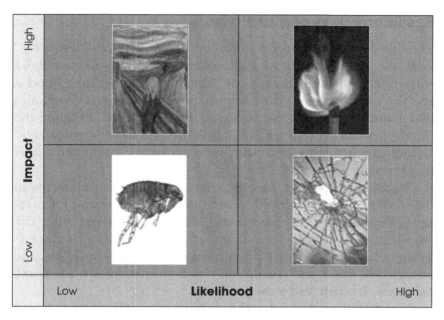

Figure 1.2   Fears, Fires, Fleas, and Flaw

Fears ("The Scream") image: ©2008 The Munch Museum/The Munch-Ellingsen Group/Artists Rights Society (ARS), NY; Fleas image: ©iStockphoto.com/Oliver Sun Kim; Fires (match flame) image: ©iStockphoto.com/Sille Van Landschoot; Flaws (broken window) image: ©iStockphoto.com/David H. Lewis.

2007 and later years, when stock option backdating risks became prominent.

The next step in devising a strategy is to consider the fraud and corruption risks in their four quadrants representing both the likelihood of their occurrence and the significance of their impact on a company-by-company basis.

The "Fears, Fires, Fleas, and Flaws" chart in Figure 1.2 represents the four quadrants of the fraud and corruption risk heat map, characterized by the nature of the risks in each.

This type of chart helps us visualize existing and emerging fraud risks more clearly *from a strategic point of view*. We will discuss this chart in much more detail in Chapter 5, but we wanted to introduce it to you now because the concept it represents is central to one of our basic premises, which can be stated simply:

> Fraud risks can be categorized in a way that makes it clear that different fraud risk management strategies may be employed for each.

Resiliency as a corporate goal

The title of this book begins with the words "Corporate Resiliency." Why did we choose the word "resiliency" as a way to describe a corporate goal? Partly because we understand that fighting fraud is always a catchup game. More importantly, we know that companies that genuinely prepare themselves to deal with fraud, meaning the frauds they can prevent and those that they will have to react to and contain, are generally successful and are a more appropriate model for corporate success.

We will suggest that, broadly, there are four basic elements to the strategies to be deployed by industry and by company, for managing the categories of risks identified in heat maps and other risk visualization devices. We maintain that these four elements can collectively lead companies toward resiliency. Roughly speaking, the elements of fraud and corruption risk management are *assessment, prevention, detection,* and *response.*

We will define the connection between these four elements and the goal of resiliency and corporate success in the remainder of this book. For now we provide a brief overview.

Performing a competent fraud and corruption risk assessment is the key first step to fraud risk management. Before putting preventive or detection strategies in place, it is necessary to identify, categorize, and assess risks, on the one hand, and to determine which risks require mitigation and what mitigation strategies to use, on the other.

Second, and based on the fraud and corruption risk assessment, is putting in place preventive strategies. There are a number of them, ranging from enterprise-wide, non-fraud-specific strategies, such as corporate ethics policies, to highly targeted controls designed to prevent specific fraud schemes. Preventive strategies prefigure actual frauds by focusing on elements of enterprise-wide measures, such as avowals by corporate leaders that misrepresentations are off-limits, and other measures designed to discourage or prevent the occurrence of specific frauds.

Third, detection strategies, which vary from periodic auditing to continuous monitoring of transactions and relationships, can selectively be put in place depending on the fraud risks identified by the company. For most companies, detection strategies will fall along a spectrum between after-the-fact sampling of selected transactions and the continuous examination of all transactions in real time.

It is worth noting that detection strategies are meant both to deter frauds, due to employees knowing they are in place, and to uncover those that occur. Clearly, the limiting factor of detection strategies lies in the fact that we can test only for schemes we know about in detail.

Finally, companies can develop response strategies designed to minimize the impact of frauds that occur, are discovered, and come to the attention of the company, authorities, and other interested parties. The response strategies include the capability to conduct sound investigations.

Response strategies occupy a wide range, varying from feedback loop techniques for updating risk analyses and detection programs, on the one hand. Then to the ability to quickly respond to discovery requests from regulators and others, and to policies relating to corporate self-investigation and disclosure to the Board, shareholders, and regulators and law enforcement officials, on the other.

We maintain that deploying these strategies collectively will put companies on the path of resiliency in regard to the threat of fraud and corruption.

CHAPTER

The Growing Risk of Fraud and Corruption

Key points:

➤ Globalization exposes businesses to more and different fraud and corruption risks.

➤ Economic uncertainty resulting from current trends will pressure more people to commit fraud.

➤ Advanced digital information technologies have created more fraud risks.

➤ Many companies are still using yesterday's techniques to fight today's fraud and corruption risks. How can they reasonably expect to cope with the risks of tomorrow?

Why should my company be especially concerned about fraud and corruption now?

Four current trends suggest that the level of fraud risk facing many companies has increased significantly.

1. Globalization

As many companies expand around the world to source supplies from other countries, or to expand their sales in emerging markets, they may encounter complex risks for which they may not be prepared.

These risks range from bribery and corruption, to compliance with export controls and anti-money-laundering statutes, to product quality risks that can endanger customers.

It should also be noted that enforcement by the U.S. Department of Justice of the Foreign Corrupt Practices Act (FCPA) has also increased dramatically.

Globalization, in other words, increases the fraud risk management pressures on multinational companies. Each market relationship poses distinct risks that must be taken into account when developing risk strategies.

Where are some of these risks? Christian Kammer, senior forensic accountant at the Integrity Vice Presidency Unit of the World Bank, suggests, "in the fast-emerging developing countries there is a lot of investment in markets that are not very well scrutinized, especially in terms of infrastructure." He adds, "the checks and balances are relatively low and therefore the opportunity for government officials and corrupt companies to collude to skim off certain amounts is really very high."

2. Economic downturns

Downturns in the economy, such as the global recession that followed the crash of 2008 can make it more difficult for executives and managers to achieve planned results. It also puts more employees under personal financial pressure.

Fraud specialists suggest that economic pressures increase the likelihood and the number of individuals resorting to fraud to achieve corporate objectives or to meet personal needs. Financial losses due to fraud are additional costs that companies will have a hard time absorbing, especially in down points in the economic cycle.

3. Risk management surprises

From the boom in mortgage fraud to the "rogue trader" and Ponzi scheme cases, recent events suggest that even companies with well-articulated risk management programs in place can be vulnerable to fraud and other business risks. Some past assumptions about risk management and fraud risk assessments may now be obsolete as changes in the economic environment, new technologies and shifting patterns of organized criminal activity drive different fraud priorities.

When stock option abuses hit the news a few years ago, the risk assessments for many companies did not identify stock option management, and issues like backdating, as high in risk. Instead, the crisis took many companies by surprise and necessitated rethinking risks.

While technology has helped us run our businesses more efficiently and created new and better fraud-monitoring capabilities, it has also added a level of complexity and exposure to fraud risk management. The interconnection of companies and their reliance on the Internet have made them more vulnerable to attack from the outside.

Similarly, the rise of the data privacy movement and the complex laws surrounding the protection of personally identifiable information, in conjunction with the increased connectivity between units of global companies, pose new challenges from a fraud risk perspective.

4. Less-than-optimal performance by many companies in managing fraud risks

Certain evidence suggests that current fraud risk management programs at many companies need improvement. A 2007 survey by the Deloitte Forensic Center, *Ten Things About Fraud Control*, revealed a substantial "fraud control gap" between companies with more effective anti-fraud programs in place and those operating with less effective anti-fraud measures.

Moreover, even for the companies considered more effective in detecting and preventing fraud, the executives surveyed believed that significant opportunities to enhance their performance continue to exist.

Recognizing the importance of sound risk management policies, Standard and Poor's (S&P) Rating Services announced in May 2008 that it would begin including an evaluation of enterprise risk management as a component of its independent credit ratings and credit analysis for nonfinancial companies, building on its experience doing this with financial companies.

We believe that the mere existence of risk management programs and anti-fraud controls may give some companies a false sense of confidence. So now may be the right time for companies to re-evaluate their programs and determine whether they are sufficiently detailed to withstand new complexities, new fraud risks, and external scrutiny.

Based on the survey results and our experience with anti-fraud programs and controls, we have identified a number of key areas, which we explore in the balance of this book, where most companies can improve their fraud risk management programs, including the following. We invite you to consider how your company is doing on each:

1. Fraud and corruption risk assessment
2. Fraud and corruption control policy
3. Employee fraud awareness training and surveys
4. Hotline benchmarking
5. Monitoring of third-party relationships in the supply chain
6. Monitoring payments, revenue, and other financial transactions
7. Investigative response plan

Local problems, global pain

To be perfectly fair, not everyone agrees with the idea that fraud and corruption risks have changed fundamentally over the past several years. Some experts take a more nuanced approach, saying the problem is less about new risks and more about the wider distribution of longstanding risks.

"It's not so much that the risks have changed," says our colleague, Tim Phillipps, Deloitte Australia partner and Asia-Pacific Forensic and Dispute Services practice leader. "The big change has been in the way many countries—particularly the U.S.—have cracked down on fraud and corruption. This worldwide trend directly affects multinational companies. Today, local problems cause global pain. Let's say you are a multinational and your corporate headquarters is in Iowa. If you have a subsidiary in the Far East and someone there is accused of bribery, the U.S. government will be calling you to find out what is going on. That is the big difference from years ago, when the problem would more likely have been contained to the region in which it occurred."

One result of this trend has been a greater awareness of new vulnerabilities stemming from fraud and corruption risks in other parts of the world. Sometimes the risks can be apparent; sometimes they are less immediately obvious, says Phillipps. In one instance, a U.S.-based multinational company invested in an Asian firm without performing a comprehensive background check. Later, the multi-national discovered that the Asian firm had a business relationship with Cuba (a serious issue due to U.S. sanctions). Although this particular case was a compliance rather than a fraud and corruption issue, the potential financial and reputational damage is not dissimilar and the apparent cause, due diligence procedures, is the same.

In this case, the multinational withdrew its investment in the Asian firm, but not before wasting significant amounts of time, money, and effort. It also lost the competitive market advantage it had originally gained when entering into the partnership, and was forced to repeat the process of finding a new Asian business partner.

Local problems can put global strategies at risk, and cause worldwide reputational damage as well, cautions Phillipps. "Reputational risk requires a new kind of due diligence. Call it 'reputational due diligence,' if you will. When your business partners have problems, those problems can become your problems very quickly."

"Companies are more vulnerable now," says Ed Rial, Deloitte Financial Advisory Services LLP principal and global leader of Deloitte's FCPA consulting practice. "In the wake of corporate scandals such as Enron and WorldCom, there has been much greater emphasis on corporate transparency and much greater accountability at senior levels. Companies are discovering corruption problems in their operations abroad and are reporting them to the government in the hope of getting reduced liability."

But there's another factor, too. "Other countries are really getting on the stick about corruption as well," Ed says. "For many years, the U.S. stood alone in many ways in combating payments to foreign officials to gain business advantages. Now many European and Latin American countries as well as a fair number of Asian countries have signed on to treaties and have enacted FCPA-like statutes. We're beginning to see greater interest from them enforcing their own anti-bribery statutes."

When you put those factors together, according to Ed, "All of a sudden FCPA and corruption has come to the forefront and represents a major concern for a company doing business abroad."

The good news is that this change helps to level the playing field for businesses around the globe, so it can help to open markets and create more opportunities for companies that operate with integrity.

Awareness is crucial

Knowledge is the first step in creating a genuine awareness of fraud risk and the starting point for developing the operational strategies that your company requires for combating fraud.

"Some companies just are not aware of the risks; they do not understand yet that they are vulnerable." says our colleague Adam Weisman. "If they were aware of the risks they are facing, they might act differently. It is like the difference between driving your car on a bright sunny day and driving your car on a dark stormy night. During the day you might listen to the radio, chat with your passengers or even enjoy a little sightseeing. If you are driving at night during a rainstorm, you are going to turn off the radio, hunch your shoulders, lean forward and concentrate on the road ahead of you."

Despite the sheer number of identifiable frauds, the truth is that fraud risks can be divided into distinct groups. Focused operational strategies can be developed and deployed to deal effectively with each group of fraud risks.

Ongoing processes can be designed and implemented to limit the scope and impact of fraud, and to reduce the likelihood of fraud recurring.

When advising clients, our colleague, Mohammed Ahmed, usually takes a minute to note that they probably already have some of the key processes we recommend in place. The issue, he says, is to fill in the gaps and round the programs and processes into the right strategic whole.

At the heart of these processes is a large amount of common sense and practical business wisdom. For example, even the most sophisticated fraud-monitoring tools generate false positives on a regular basis. Your company's knowledge of its past history of fraud—and its ability to spot the difference between an out-of-pattern data point and a red flag—will be crucial to the overall success of your fraud risk management strategies.

A company that understands its past experience with fraud, warts and all, will be in a better position to deal effectively with fraud when it arises in the future.

Understanding and acknowledging past experiences with fraud requires a fairly high level of candor and transparency, and the fact is that greater transparency is associated with superior business results. From our perspective, the ability to deal effectively with fraud issues is both a core competency and a hallmark of management excellence.

Most important, we believe that the ability to deal with fraud on a continuous basis and to minimize its potential for harm is a strong indicator of organizational health. It is also one of the hallmarks of a resilient corporation.

Common sense and observable reality

Once you accept the premise that the "infinite variety" of individual fraud events can be parsed into a manageable number of categories, it becomes possible to devise methodologies for identifying fraud risks, predicting the likelihood of their occurrence, implementing tactics to monitor and detect fraud schemes, and developing appropriate response processes for minimizing damage and guarding against recurrence.

In this book, we present what we believe are today's leading practices in fraud risk management. Our goals are to raise your awareness, provide an actionable framework for managing fraud risks, and share general examples that illustrate how various companies have dealt successfully (or unsuccessfully) with incidents of fraud.

It is important to begin with a broad understanding of the current environment. Fraud is not evenly distributed across the economy.

Some types of fraud occur with greater frequency in some sectors than in others. Certain types of fraud occur more often in the retail industry than in the financial services or telecommunications industries. Other types of fraud occur more commonly in the healthcare industry than in the manufacturing sector.

"In some regions of the world, people still do much of their business on a cash basis. Companies are small and one or two people often hold multiple roles. So there is little or no separation of duties. These circumstances can create temptations", says Dr. Olivier Brasseur, director of the Division for Oversight Services at the United Nations Population Fund.

Tailoring efforts to avert damage

It is clear that fraud has a chameleon-like quality. Those who commit fraud show no lack of imagination in customizing schemes to work in new or different environments.

There is also a general relationship between the level of those who commit fraud, the type of fraud, and the resulting monetary loss. This is well documented in the Association of Certified Fraud Examiners' *2008 Report to the Nation on Occupational Fraud and Abuse.*

For example, the report shows that those engaging in asset-misappropriation schemes, are more likely to be lower-level employees while those manipulating financial statements are more likely to be business owners or executives higher levels are generally more likely to be involved in manipulating financial statements.

The fact that certain types of fraud occur more frequently in some industries and less frequently in others, and that certain types of fraud occur more frequently at different levels of the company, actually works to the advantage of management, since it makes the job of targeting specific types of fraud easier.

In other words, instead of worrying about every conceivable kind of fraud under the sun, you begin by concentrating on the types of fraud most likely to occur in your industry and at your company, and you tailor your anti-fraud efforts to focus on the levels within the company where fraudulent activities can inflict the most damage. That, however, is just the beginning.

CHAPTER 3

The Costs of Fraud and Corruption

Key points:

➤ Despite recent legislation and an increased emphasis on anti-fraud controls, U.S. companies are estimated in an ACFE survey to lose 7 percent of their annual revenues to fraud.

➤ The long-term impact of fraud and corruption is broad and extensive, casting a shadow on future earnings and value creation.

➤ The downside risks of fraud and corruption cannot be measured in purely monetary terms.

➤ The Internet and other new media virtually guarantee that bad news will spread globally like wildfire, creating more risks for companies when they experience fraud.

➤ Business executives convicted of fraud can expect to serve time in prison.

Higher stakes

Measuring the extent of fraud and corruption is inherently difficult as it is purposely concealed by perpetrators and rarely tracked separately in corporate accounting systems. But media stories, prosecutions, government reports and private sector studies provide insights into the perceived scale of the problem.

For example, the Association of Certified Fraud Examiners (ACFE) conducts a fraud survey of its members every two years. Most of the survey inquires about anonymized descriptive data from cases members have investigated. But the ACFE also asks each survey participant to provide his or her best estimate of the percentage of annual revenues lost by the typical U.S. organization to fraud each year. In its *2008 Report to the Nation on Occupational Fraud and Abuse,* the ACFE reports that the median response from the nearly 1,000 anti-fraud professionals participating indicated that the typical U.S. company loses seven percent of its annual revenues to fraudulent activity. This is an increase from the five percent in the ACFE's previous report published in 2006. In reports from 1996 to 2004, the loss was consistently estimated at 6 percent of revenues.

The ACFE emphasizes that this estimate, "is based solely on the opinions of CFEs [certified fraud examiners] who are in the trenches fighting fraud on a daily basis, rather than on any specific data or factual observations. Thus, this figure should not be considered a literal representation of the true cost of fraud facing U.S. organizations." At the same time, they say, "the 7 percent figure is a meaningful and insightful estimate that may be as close to a reliable measure of the cost of fraud as one can get. The figure provides a best-guess point of reference based on the opinions of 959 anti-fraud experts with a median of 15 years' experience in the prevention and detection of occupational fraud."

The ACFE reports that seven percent of U.S. gross domestic product would amount to an estimated $994 billion in fraud-related losses for 2008 across the U.S. economy as a whole. We can say that while some of this might be observable in the form of large credit card fraud, insurance fraud, healthcare fraud and loan fraud losses recorded by companies in certain industries, much would be invisible, absorbed into the cost of goods and services businesses and consumers purchase every day.

Other data in the ACFE's *2008 Report to the Nation on Occupational Fraud and Abuse* is based not on opinion but on the analysis of data from 959 cases of occupational fraud that were investigated between January 2006 and February 2008. All the information was provided by the CFEs who investigated those cases.

The ACFE reported that the median loss caused by each fraud in its study was $175,000. More than one-quarter of the frauds involved losses of at least $1 million. The typical fraud lasted two years before it was uncovered.

Figure 3.1 compares the distribution of fraud losses in the ACFE's 2006 and 2008 reports.

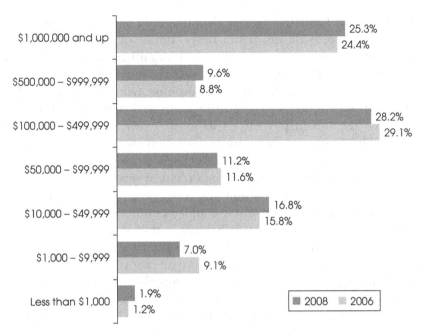

Figure 3.1   This chart from the ACFE's 2008 Report to the Nation shows the distribution of dollar losses in the fraud cases studied

Fraud is not only costly but can be hard to recover from. In other words, fraud has a direct impact on the bottom line. A company with a 10 percent profit margin that experiences a single $250,000 misappropriation of assets would have to generate an additional $2.5 million in revenue to restore its net income to pre-fraud levels. In today's competitive marketplace, generating that additional revenue may be difficult.

These numbers are not trivial, especially when you project them across the width and breadth of the economy. But in a very real sense, they are only part of a much larger tapestry because they represent only *today's* losses.

Casting a shadow on the future

Ongoing fraud and corruption schemes represent a continuing drain on a company's profitability. Shutting down frauds and removing or reducing the opportunity for similar schemes to be

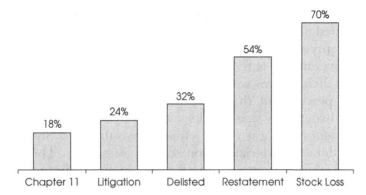

Figure 3.2 Fraction of companies issued an AAER with various adverse events

perpetrated in future can enhance profitability not only in the current year but also for years to come.

Companies that experience financial statement fraud in their operations may also experience a variety of other potentially costly events subsequently, whether caused by the fraud or by other factors impacting at the same time. In 2008, the Deloitte Forensic Center (DFC) completed a study of Accounting and Auditing Enforcement Releases (AAERs) issued by the U.S. Securities and Exchange Commission (SEC), which the SEC publishes when they allege a company to have engaged in accounting fraud.

It was clear from the study that the experiences of these companies vary considerably.

From 2000 through 2007, the SEC pursued enforcement actions related to 352 companies for financial statement fraud. The DFC determined the incidence of certain events for these companies, namely financial statement restatements, Chapter 11 bankruptcy filings, and primary exchange delistings, and determined the magnitude of securities class-action litigation settlements and declines in stock value. See Figure 3.2.

Of the companies subject to financial statement fraud AAERs, 54 percent issued restatements of their financial statement results with 96 percent of those restatements having an overall negative financial impact on the company's results.

The inter-correlations of the different events observed are also of interest. Of the 54 percent of companies alleged by the SEC to have committed financial statement fraud and which restated, 20 percent filed for Chapter 11 of these United States Bankruptcy Code. Twenty-eight percent of the companies that restated their financial statements were also delisted from the primary exchange on which their shares were traded. In addition, more than one-third (37 percent) of the companies faced securities class-action litigations brought by shareholders.

Twenty-four percent of the companies subject to SEC actions settled Federal Court class-action security litigations. The average settlement amount in these cases, for the 354 companies facing SEC allegations and which were sued, was $286 million. That number includes small number of "outliers" or unusually large settlements. Excluding the top three and bottom three companies in order of settlement size leads to an average settlement of $118 million.

The results of the study also show a positive correlation between the number of fraud schemes alleged by the SEC at each company and both (1) the likelihood of having to defend against a federal securities class action and (2) the size of the settlements in such litigations.

In its AAERs, the SEC details each fraud scheme they allege in a company. Analyzing the AAERs we found that 78 percent of the companies subject to AAERs had more than one accounting fraud scheme alleged for the period of the SEC investigation.

Interestingly, 7 percent of the companies had more than 10 alleged fraud schemes, and 4 companies had more than 20. We note that the companies with more than ten schemes settled filed litigations for substantially greater amounts. These statistics suggest that those performing fraud risk assessments and investigations be open to the possibility that multiple fraud schemes may be present at one time in a given company and that controlling these has significant implications regarding possible downside effects for companies.

Seventy percent of the publicly-traded companies accused of financial statement fraud saw their stock price drop between the date of the outset of the fraud and the date of the SEC's action. More than half of those companies experienced a decrease in stock value of greater than 50 percent, and 35 percent experienced a loss ranging between 75 percent and 100 percent.

A variety of factors will influence stock price changes over these periods, often lasting several years, so they cannot be attributed to the fraud. Companies experiencing financial statement fraud are often also experiencing significant operational and marketplace difficulties and perhaps management challenges in parts of their organization, which can impact their results, future prospects and share price. Whatever the precise reasons for the stock price changes, in the majority of cases the direction is unlikely to please investors.

Cost and availability of capital

Two recent developments suggest that the time may be coming when companies with weak risk management capabilities experience greater difficulty in obtaining capital and have to pay a higher risk premium.

The announcement by Standard and Poor's that it will factor certain aspects of risk management into companies' credit ratings starting in 2009 has the potential to create greater differentiation in the marketplace between those companies that have stronger risk management capabilities and those that are weaker. The ability to look "under the hood" and identify such differences could be highly valuable to lenders, enabling them to better identify potential sources of credit risk. At the same time, it could reward companies with stronger risk management capabilities by leading to a lower cost of capital.

The second development stems directly from the financial crisis that began in 2008. Our colleague Humphry Hatton, leader of the Forensic and Dispute Services practice for Deloitte UK, says, "Right now the banks have lost their appetite for lending. But when they do start, they're going to be looking at this issue more carefully. A company that is susceptible to fraud, or whose controls the markets believe to be weak, is likely to find it harder to raise money than before the credit crunch hit. I think we should expect there to be some real financial penalty embedded in the control environment."

With a number of major financial institutions reporting substantial potential losses from the alleged $50 billion fraud at Bernard L. Madoff Investment Securities LLC, their sensitivity to fraud risks may well be enhanced. Whether the risk premium discussed above arises quickly with the new credit rating system or takes more time, the direction appears to be set. Greater emphasis on corporate risk management capabilities seems likely for the future.

Bad news travels even faster than before

As mentioned earlier, the downside risks of fraud cannot be measured in purely monetary terms. The proliferation of cable news outlets, web-based news portals, blogs, RSS feeds, text messaging, and dozens of other "new media" platforms means that news (especially bad news) travels faster than ever.

As Martin Biegelman, director of the Financial Integrity Unit for Microsoft Corporation, puts it, "In today's shrinking world, a whisper uttered in New York is heard in Beijing, and a deal made in Delhi is felt in London."

It is fair to say that we have entered an era of "instantaneous" trial by fire. Today, the court of public opinion does not wait for the evening news; it is ready to pass sentence any time of day or night.

For companies or individuals implicated in fraud, the 24/7 news cycle is more than a nuisance. It is a source of steady, intense pressure that can lead to harsh consequences.

Remember the fate of Arthur Andersen LLP. The firm effectively vanished in 2002 after being convicted of a felony in connection with the Enron scandal. The U.S. Supreme Court's 2005 reversal of the conviction came too late to save Andersen.

Don't expect a slap on the wrist

Since July 2002, the Department of Justice has obtained nearly 1,300 corporate fraud convictions, according to a presidential report issued by the Corporate Fraud Task Force in 2008. These figures include convictions of more than 200 chief executive officers and corporate presidents, more than 120 corporate vice presidents, and more than 50 chief financial officers, the report noted.

C-suite corporate officers are not the only ones feeling the heat. In 2007, a record number of general counsels "were charged with or pleaded to civil or criminal fraud in federal courts, most in the wake of the stock-options backdating scandal," according to the *National Law Journal.*

Corporate fines and penalties are setting records. In 2007, a U.S. engineering company pleaded guilty to violating the Foreign Corrupt Practices Act and agreed to pay $44.1 million in penalties and forfeitures, which the government said was the largest penalty ever for violations of the act. But this seemed relatively small

	FY 2005	FY 2006	FY 2007
Investigations Initiated	102	40	124
Prosecution Recommendations	115	76	77
Indictments/Information	69	78	53
Sentenced	51	36	51
Incarceration Rate	80.4%	86.1%	68.6%
Avg. Months to Serve	23	49	20

Figure 3.3   Those Convicted of Fraud Can Expect Prison Time
Source: Corporate Fraud Task Force Report.

by 2008, when a European engineering company pleaded guilty to violating U.S. anti-corruption laws and agreed to pay $1.6 billion to settle bribery inquiries in the United States and Germany.

Clearly, there is evidence of a trend toward more aggressive enforcement of anti-corporate fraud and anti-corruption laws, and a far greater willingness to seek punishment for convicted malefactors.

But it is also important for executives to understand how many separate agencies investigate corporate fraud. In addition to the Department of Justice, the Department of the Treasury, and the Securities and Exchange Commission, suspected occurrences of corporate fraud and corruption are investigated by the Department of Labor, the Federal Communications Commission, the Commodity Futures Trading Commission, the U.S. Postal Inspection Service, and the Department of Energy, not to mention officials in state and local offices, officials from other countries, and so forth.

Inside many of these agencies are smaller units with investigatory powers. For example, within the Department of the Treasury, the Internal Revenue Service's Criminal Investigations Division focuses on fighting corporate fraud.

The resources of all these various federal agencies — combined with hundreds of state and local agencies charged with enforcing laws against fraud and corruption — represents truly formidable powers that should be taken seriously.

Fraud should no longer be considered some kind of inferior crime that rates a mere slap on the wrist. Legal jurisdictions all over the world have demonstrated that they are willing, and some would say eager, to enforce laws against fraud and to sentence convicted violators to prison terms.

So, as well as the costs borne by corporations and their shareholders when fraud is committed, there are severe personal costs to be considered. Prosecutors are likely to hold senior executives accountable. Defense attorneys are expensive, prison is a very real potential prospect, and even if you win your day in court, the cost, strain and reputational impact of defending yourself in a criminal trial can be substantial.

The decline in the incarceration rate reported for Fiscal Year (FY) 2007 is the result of a larger number of sentenced cases identified as a corporate entity in the FY 2007 data, when compared to FY 2006. Corporate entities do not incur months to serve, and therefore reduce the incarceration rate.

As Figure 3.3 from the Corporate Fraud Task Force report unmistakably shows, those convicted of fraud can expect to serve time in prison.

PART 2

ON BECOMING RESILIENT: STRATEGIES FOR AVOIDING AND MINIMIZING THE IMPACT OF FRAUD AND CORRUPTION

4

Building a Resilient Corporation

Key points:

➤ In today's complex environment, fraud and corruption risks are virtually impossible to avoid completely.

➤ Resilient corporations develop effective strategies for preventing, detecting, and responding to fraud and corruption.

➤ Traditional methods for combating fraud and corruption can be updated with newer strategies that are focused, flexible, and relevant.

➤ Resiliency is both an achievable and a necessary goal; successful companies are likely to view resiliency as a competitive asset.

What determines survivability?

Even in the worst natural disasters, it always seems as if one or two buildings remain standing amid the rubble. Why is this? What quality is it that enables them to avoid collapsing when everything around them lies in ruin?

By the same token, why do some companies survive major incidents of fraud or corruption while others fold under the strain? What quality is it that enables them to stay in business, to recover their equilibrium, to regroup and to move on?

These questions form the subtext of everything in this book. Why do some companies disintegrate in the face of fraud? How do other companies absorb the shock and manage to keep going? In fact, our study of companies accused of financial statement fraud by the SEC shows that some companies not only weather the storm but also enhance share values.

What sets the survivors apart? What are their special characteristics? Why are they so resilient, and how did they get that way?

Reducing vulnerability

If we accept the idea that fraud cannot be eliminated completely, then a realistic definition of success would be the ability of a company to reduce vulnerability and increase its capacity to bounce back from a potential disaster.

Resiliency is the quality of returning to form following stress. This definition comes loosely from the engineering world. In the context of corporate entities, a return to form following the stress of fraud means a continued focus on key business principles. This means a successful focus on the market, on levels of profitability, and so forth, combined with timely and effectively restoring confidence in the company by customers, regulators, employees, and other key stakeholders.

Traits of a resilient corporation

In the neurosciences, *resiliency* is now recognized as a descriptive concept differentiating those victims of head injuries associated with post traumatic stress syndrome who recover more readily from those who do not.

In social policy, resiliency is the quality that enables nations or regions to bounce back quickly from catastrophe. The key societal characteristic are adequate planning and social investment in things like warning systems, strong, enforced building codes, disaster recovery measures, and adequate attention to the medical requirements disasters generate.

In other words, resiliency can be viewed as doing the things necessary to minimize harmful effects and mobilize resources to facilitate recovery.

The resilient corporation neither neglects the possibility of fraud nor attempts to build an impermeable wall against it. Instead, the resilient corporation erects a practical anti-fraud framework, informed by a competent fraud risk assessment, and comprised of the three fundamental strategies: *prevention, detection,* and *response.*

Three key characteristics of resiliency

As suggested above, the characteristics of resilient corporations, like those of resilient people and resilient nations, allow them to avoid problems by limiting the incidence of fraud, by reducing their vulnerability to fraud events, and by limiting the impact of fraud. More specifically, such companies put policies in place, whether self-consciously or not, that work to achieve these objectives:

1. *Avoiding problems* through adequate planning and the installation of policies and procedures (e.g., establishing an ethical corporate culture, or avoiding certain high-risk areas of business) that limit the incidence of fraud
2. *Reduction of vulnerabilities* by focusing on early warning of problems (e.g., employing detection mechanisms) and establishing policies to address problems identified
3. *Limiting impact* by establishing policies and procedures prior to the event that help effect a quick return to business (e.g., identification of problems via internal investigations and self-reporting)

Why resiliency is achievable

Forensic accounting specialists, fraud examiners, regulators, law enforcement officials, corporate governance specialists, academics, and others have learned an enormous amount about fraud and corruption schemes. This includes both how fraud schemes work and methods that can be used to avoid and minimize them. This community of experts has developed significant literature, a body of knowledge, and canon of guidance regarding fraud and corruption risk management.

This knowledge and guidance creates an opportunity to adopt corporate practices that foster resiliency. Without it, the task of fraud avoidance and recovery would be much more daunting than it is. Our goal is to present the available knowledge, as well as our own experience, in a way that will enable executives to ask key questions about the state of the fraud avoidance at their companies and to guide their companies toward robust policies that put them on the path of corporate resiliency.

Why Resiliency?

Resiliency is usually defined as the ability of a person or organization to adjust to events, especially those relating to misfortune or change. We suggest that fraud risk management is really about fostering resiliency in regard to fraud and corruption risks, and that corporations would be well-served to adopt the goal of developing the ability to avoid and to adjust to fraud and corruption risks by embracing the key strategies outlined in this book.

The strategies are easy to describe. They begin with, or are predicated on, competent risk assessments. Following from there, they can include strategies designed to help corporations avoid fraud, strategies designed to watch out for and detect the frauds that occur, and response strategies, like internal investigation capabilities, designed to limit the damage that instances of fraud and corruption can inflict.

Accepting the key premise that we cannot eradicate fraud and corruption, the argument of this book is that we can, through appropriate measures, reduce the likelihood of their occurrence and/or minimize their effects on our companies. We can, in other words, help companies become resilient to the risk of fraud and corruption.

Learn from the experience of others

As we will emphasize in the next chapter, the existing professional literature and guidance on anti-fraud risk assessment methods and objectives form a particularly important part of an overall strategy for managing fraud risk. As Chapters 6, 7, and 8 will make clear, this literature and guidance couples closely with key fraud avoidance techniques, such as the imperatives to create ethical corporate cultures, employee testing and screening, and whistle-blower or tipster policies, on the one hand, and active anti-fraud monitoring and detection techniques, on the other.

The experience of professionals involved in fraud examination and investigation provides significant guidance regarding the question of policies that would desirably be in place to help companies when frauds are suspected or revealed. This guidance ranges from the question of what would be included in a corporate investigation function to when to engage outside assistance as well as when to self-report to regulators and law enforcement officials.

While techniques to combat fraud go back some decades, and guidance has become increasingly knowledge based, concern about anti-corruption is more recent. Still, an increased focus on the effects of corruption by international organizations, developed countries, and nongovernmental organizations (NGOs) has led to the development of due diligence techniques and policies designed to combat official corruption.

Putting in place the policies the guidance suggests and realizing the goal of becoming resilient requires ongoing preventative measures. This includes the development and nurturing of an ethical corporate culture; the implementation of corporate governance, risk, and compliance processes; and a working system of anti-fraud controls, as well as developing robust processes for anti-fraud monitoring, investigation, and mitigation.

By way of summary, a practical fraud risk avoidance and mitigation framework might resemble Figure 4.1.

What are the benefits of fraud and corruption risk management?

Strong fraud and corruption risk management makes good business sense. In our experience, companies that implement detailed fraud and corruption risk management processes can also experience related benefits, including:

- Reduced financial losses due to fraud and corruption
- Reduced costs of responding to fraud and corruption (investigations, legal costs, and regulatory enforcements)
- Assist in complying with applicable U.S. and other regulatory requirements, such as the Sarbanes-Oxley Act and its foreign counter-parts such as Japan's "J-SOX" and Canada's "CSOX", the Foreign Corrupt Practices Act, USA Patriot Act, U.S. sentencing guidelines, and the Organization for Economic Co-operation and Development (OECD) anti-corruption measures, among others
- Enhanced ethical culture ("tone at the top") supporting recruitment and retention of high-quality employees
- Increased reporting of potential frauds and other ethical issues
- More effective corporate governance and the potential for improved governance ratings

Executives from companies considered to be more effective at fraud control, surveyed for *Ten Things About Fraud Control,* anticipated

Fraud and Corruption Risk Governance

- Establishes management responsibilities and processes for oversight by those charged with governance
- Sets fraud and corruption risk tolerance, risk management goals, performance measures, and evaluation processes

Fraud and Corruption Risk Assessment

- Designed to identify and evaluate potential fraud and corruption risks
- Supports business process owners and those charged with overseeing risk management
- Serves as a deterrent by exploring new and emerging risks

Risk Avoidance and Mitigation

Preventive Controls	**Detective Controls**
• Designed to mitigate the opportunity for an individual to perpetrate a fraud	• Designed to identify indicators of a fraud, if committed
• Limited effectiveness when management may be involved in the fraud	• May be used as a monitoring activity to assess effectiveness of other anti-fraud controls
• Serve as a deterrent by creating an additional obstacle to carrying out a fraud	• Serve as a deterrent by heightening the perceived likelihood of being caught

Investigation and Remediation

- Designed to resolve issues and remediate business processes and controls
- Effectiveness enhanced through advance preparation of protocols and identification of key investigative resources to be used
- Serves as a deterrent by creating an expectation of diligent investigation of alleged or suspected fraud and corruption

Figure 4.1   Sample Fraud Avoidance and Mitigation Framework

that instances of fraud were much less likely to occur over the next 12 months as compared with companies with less effective fraud controls.

Since fraud risks can have serious financial and reputational consequences, potential risk reductions in these areas should be especially valuable to companies, their directors, and their officers.

Real World Example

Prior to establishing a claims investigation group, a company annually paid out millions of dollars relating to insurance claims, many of which were false. After establishing an anti-fraud investigation group, the company saved millions of dollars annually in false claims, thus repaying the cost of the group many times over.

Hugh Hooker, chief compliance officer for Petro-Canada, describes the value of a proactive approach to fraud and corruption risk management this way: "A reactive response is usually much more expensive and you are risking already having suffered damage to your reputation. So we much prefer a proactive approach and have been able to convince our executives that a proactive approach works. Proactive is safer and ultimately less costly."

Convincing senior executives of the value of proactive fraud and corruption risk management is sometimes more art than science. Martin Biegelman, director of the Financial Integrity Unit at Microsoft Corporation, describes it this way: "I like to say if the vivid and disturbing images of former CEOs and CFOs being led away in handcuffs isn't convincing enough, I don't know what is. That's an ultimate penalty." As he puts it, "senior executives who have integrity and honesty as core values, who truly believe in accountability and transparency, who know that the tone at the top means both talk and action on an ongoing basis, need no further convincing."

Christian Kammer, senior forensic accountant at the Integrity Vice Presidency Unit of the World Bank, describes the value this way: "It does actually make financial sense in terms of return on investment if you are able to flag the fraud problems that the company has had and the benefits that they may have from putting in place an internal investigation and a fraud prevention and compliance program for the future." He adds, "If you have a good reputation, people are more likely to look at you and want to do business with you."

Five principles of fraud risk management

In July 2008, new guidance, *Managing the Business Risk of Fraud: A Practical Guide* (the "Guide"), was issued by the Institute of Internal Auditors (IIA), the American Institute of Certified Public Accountants (AICPA), and the Association of Certified Fraud Examiners (ACFE).

The Guide was developed for companies to use to help evaluate their fraud risk management processes, identify improvement opportunities, and take steps to enhance performance where it makes sense to do so. The Guide should be of strong interest to executives, boards, audit committees, internal auditors, and those involved in compliance and risk management.

The Guide sets out five core principles:

Principle 1: As part of an organization's governance structure, a fraud risk management program should be in place, including a written policy (or policies) to convey the expectations of the board of directors and senior management regarding managing fraud risk.

Principle 2: Fraud risk exposure should be assessed periodically by the organization to identify specific potential schemes and events that the organization needs to mitigate.

Principle 3: Prevention techniques to avoid potential key fraud risk events should be established, where feasible, to mitigate possible impacts on the organization.

Principle 4: Detection techniques should be established to uncover fraud events when preventive measures fail or unmitigated risks are realized.

Principle 5: A reporting process should be in place to solicit input on potential fraud, and a coordinated approach to investigation and corrective action should be used to help ensure potential fraud is addressed appropriately and timely.

The Guide emphasizes the need for a company's board of directors or other governing body to ensure that its governance practices set the tone for fraud risk management. Management's role includes implementing policies that encourage ethical behavior.

The roles and responsibilities for personnel at all levels of the company involved in fraud risk management can be defined clearly.

In addition to the Guide, Section 301 of the Sarbanes-Oxley Act, Securities & Exchange Commission rules, and the listing standards of the New York Stock Exchange and NASDAQ all address the oversight role that the board of directors, especially the audit committee, performs with regard to risk management.

The fraud risk management responsibility of those charged with governance is an important fiduciary duty that requires adequate time and resources to respond to the charge.

While many companies have a process that governs fraud risks, typical opportunities for improvement in this area might include:

- Implementing enhanced board of directors oversight of fraud risk management
- Appointing an executive-level member of management responsible for fraud risk management
- Establishing a formal fraud control policy/strategy
- Implementing risk management goals, performance measures, and periodic process evaluations
- Coordinating the efforts of different functions (e.g., internal audit, security, legal, human resources, accounting, finance, etc.) to reduce overlapping activities and address risk management gaps
- Formalizing roles and responsibilities of the board, audit committee, management, and staff related to fraud risk management

The first line of defense

While it is not possible to eliminate fraud entirely, the appropriate prevention and detection measures can significantly mitigate fraud risks.

The Guide emphasizes that fraud prevention is the first line of defense in reducing fraud risk. Companies can increase their fraud prevention efforts through continuous communication and reinforcement.

The Guide also reminds us that "one of the strongest fraud deterrents is the awareness that effective detective controls are in place."

In our experience, typical improvement opportunities in fraud prevention and detection might include:

- Improving employee fraud awareness training
- Benchmarking fraud helplines/hotlines to uncover performance issues
- Reprioritizing fraud detection efforts to give greater emphasis to the most significant fraud risks
- Greater use of technology to enhance fraud detection and deterrence

How can companies use the new guidance?

The most important message to take away from the Guide is that fraud risk management is dynamic.

As businesses change and grow, so do their fraud risks. We suggest a continuous improvement approach to fraud risk management that involves regular measurements of where the business is and where it wants to be in terms of effectively deterring, detecting, and preventing fraud.

We call this approach the *Measure, Improve, and Move Methodology*. Figure 4.2 summarizes the steps in this approach to raising performance.

Building resiliency by enhancing fraud and corruption risk management

We suggest that you make fraud and corruption risk management a renewed priority. Have a discussion about the Guide, involving your

Real World Example

Fraud detection technology helped one company detect potential fraud, waste, and abuse by flagging common bank account numbers between employees and vendors. Further investigation of these flagged accounts indicated that an employee had diverted millions of dollars in legitimate vendor payments to his own bank account. The company was able to recover the monies and remediate the access control that allowed the incidents to occur.

Evaluate	Identify Risk	Action Plan	Mitigate	Monitor	Respond
Analyze the current status and effectiveness of the approach to implementing anti-fraud programs and controls within the business	Assess, define, and document fraud risks and control effectiveness; establish fraud risk profile by analysis of risk against controls	Help prepare an action plan to address areas of fraud risk identified for control improvement or new control implementation during the fraud risk assessment	Enhance, implement, and maintain preventative and detective control activities that help mitigate fraud risks identified during the fraud risk assessment	Help enable continuous monitoring activities through an ongoing review of activities to alert management of potential fraud; incorporate findings into annual fraud risk assessment process	Assist in responding to potential occurrences of fraud within the business

Figure 4.2 Measure, Improve, and Move Methodology

Real World Example

For many years, a major international company performed audits of its employees' travel and expense claims without identifying any major frauds. However, after expanding its fraud awareness training to all overseas locations, the company received several alerts through its whistle-blower hotline. The allegations related to misuse of authority and override of controls by senior executives at an overseas location that was never subject to a full-scale internal audit due to its small size. The resulting investigation revealed corruption and serious violations of the code of conduct by senior executives at this location. Better awareness of fraud risks and an appreciation for headquarters' commitment to ethics influenced the whistle-blowers to report such activities.

senior management, board of directors, and audit committee to garner top-level support.

We encourage you to talk about fraud and corruption risks and how companies can benefit by enhancing their fraud and corruption risk management capabilities. Also, share examples of fraud schemes in the news or from your company's past—intelligent risk management comes with openness and awareness. It can be helpful to talk about frauds in other companies in your same industry. History tends to repeat itself.

We suggest that you perform a gap analysis, compare your company's fraud risk management practices with those recommended in the Guide, and identify the missing elements and determine priorities for how these gaps can be addressed.

For those practices your company already has in place, you can use the leading practices suggested in the Guide to help uncover further performance improvement opportunities. Some companies find a scorecard or a simple "red, yellow, green" rating system efficient and effective.

We encourage you to plan and execute a fraud and corruption risk management program, establishing clear roles, responsibilities, and accountability for fraud risk management and setting goals and timelines. Measure your progress in implementing improvements.

You can put an annual process in place to update the fraud and corruption risk assessment and re-evaluate your fraud and corruption risk management plan based on changes in the risk environment. Some executives find a dashboard approach helpful for monitoring and sharing information about their program.

The Guide also makes this excellent point: "Only through diligent and ongoing effort can an organization protect itself against significant acts of fraud." While preventing all fraud is unlikely to be achievable, we believe those companies that implement more effective anti-fraud processes stand a better chance of survival and success in today's riskier environment.

Corporate resiliency self-assessment tool

Now that you have had a chance to consider corporate resiliency in regard to fraud and corruption, you might want to think about where your company stands and how extensive the performance improvement opportunities might be.

This short self-assessment tool will help you assess whether your company is well on its way toward corporate resiliency with respect to fraud and corruption risks, or whether it may have some catching up to do.

These questions are not the only important ones. But they tackle some of the issues leading companies are addressing to enhance their preparedness, building their corporate resiliency to fraud and corruption risks.

For each of the 10 questions in Figure 4.3, check "No, or somewhat" or "Yes, absolutely", then total the number of responses of each type. See the "So how did you do?" section below to help you evaluate your score.

Corporate Resiliency Self-Assessment	No, or somewhat	Yes, absolutely
1.	Do management and the board of directors view effective risk management as a key enabler for informed and responsible risk-taking in the organization's operations?		
2.	Do you update your fraud and corruption risk assessment at least annually?		
3.	Does your fraud and corruption risk assessment drive action plans to reduce such risks to a tolerable level approved by the board of directors?		
4.	Is fraud and corruption risk management an explicit component of performance evaluation and compensation for executives and managers?		
5.	Do you measure employees' perceptions about the "tone at the top" and management's commitment to a workplace of integrity, using an employee survey each year?		
6.	Do you benchmark the performance of your whistle-blower hotline annually against industry-specific data for report volume, subject mix, and anonymity usage?		
7.	Do you have a crisis management plan in place with assigned responsibilities and communications plans to help drive stakeholder confidence in your response to any major issue?		
8.	Do you have a cooperative relationship with your regulators so they will be more inclined to trust and assist you in a crisis?		
9.	Have you established written protocols governing how fraud and corruption investigations will be performed?		
10.	Have you identified in advance the legal, computer forensics and forensic accounting resources you will use to conduct fraud and corruption investigations when an urgent need arises, especially for remote locations?		
	Total number of responses of each type:		

Figure 4.3 Assessment Tool

So how did you do?

10 **"Yes, absolutely" responses:** You look like a leader on the path to corporate resiliency. Don't get complacent though; there may still be fraud and corruption areas you can learn more about and improve.

7–9 **"Yes absolutely" responses:** It looks like you are doing well, with some areas for improvement. Take advantage of the opportunity to continue to raise your game in combating fraud and corruption.

4–6 **"Yes absolutely" responses:** You've made some progress on the journey to corporate resiliency. There's a way to go yet, so you might want to think about ways to accelerate your fraud and corruption risk management enhancements.

1–3 **"Yes absolutely" responses:** You've made a start. There's much to do yet. Consider putting a fraud and corruption risk management process improvement plan in place to move quickly to a much higher level of corporate resiliency.

0 **"Yes absolutely" responses:** A clean slate gives you an opportunity to implement leading fraud and corruption risk management practices, reduce your vulnerability, and build corporate resiliency. Take advantage of it while you can.

Fraud and Corruption Risk Assessment

Key points:

➢ An effective fraud and corruption risk assessment is the corner-stone of a fraud and corruption risk management program.

➢ A good fraud and corruption risk assessment serves as a valuable practical tool for the business process owners managing these risks and for the board and audit committee overseeing them.

➢ Many companies have not yet achieved a high level of sophistication in their fraud and corruption risk assessment, creating significant opportunities for improvement.

➢ Companies would desirably perform and update their risk assessments regularly to understand evolving risks and new vulnerabilities that may emerge over time.

➢ The risk of management override of internal controls is often underestimated; the board and audit committee have a key role to play in getting this robustly addressed.

Behind the facade

Regulators, judges, and other stakeholders are increasingly asking not just whether a company has an anti-fraud, anti-money-laundering, or corporate ethics policy in place, but they are also asking how well such programs work and whether their quality and results make sense. Essentially, they are asking: How good are these programs? This trend raises the stakes for everyone charged with governance responsibilities.

We believe that companies now face as great a risk of fraud and corruption as ever before. Current business trends, such as supply chain globalization and further reliance on information technology, coupled with economic instability, have increased both the pressures and the opportunities for fraud and corruption to occur.

Additionally, companies should consider the heightened public and regulatory scrutiny, and the potential for reputational damage that follows fraud and corruption allegations. In this climate, companies would be well-advised to take a fresh look at their fraud and corruption risk management practices.

This chapter provides suggestions for executives facing the practical challenges of fraud and corruption risk management process design and implementation, and especially the assessments of risk on which they are based.

What is a fraud and corruption risk assessment?

Fraud and corruption risk assessment is an integral part of any anti-fraud program that is based on the COSO framework. COSO is short for the Committee of Sponsoring Organizations of the Treadway Commission. It is a private-sector entity, the goal of which is to reduce the incidence of fraudulent financial reporting by setting standards for internal control systems.

It is also a crucial part of a company's broader risk management process, since it considers the ways that fraud and corruption can occur by and against the company.

SEC Guidance to Management related to Section 404 of the Sarbanes Oxley Act of 2002 (Release 33-8810) emphasizes the need for management to assess risks and adequacy of controls. Essentially, fraud and corruption risk assessments catalogue the frauds that could occur in business units, determine how likely they are and how material they might be, and match the risk with an action plan to control it.

How important is a good fraud and corruption risk assessment?

Performing an effective fraud and corruption risk assessment is the cornerstone of a fraud risk management program. Put simply, it's hard to have good fraud risk management if you haven't identified your fraud and corruption risks well.

Ideally, a fraud and corruption risk assessment addresses relevant key areas and is tailored to the company's size, complexity, industry, and goals. Cookie-cutter risk assessments or those copied from other companies might generate a lot of output quickly but there is no substitute for actually thinking about your own company's risks.

Hugh Hooker, chief compliance officer for Petro-Canada, describes how his company evaluates risks prior to entering new international markets. As an energy company, their business can take them to parts of the world where risks are often greater. He says, "Before we enter any country, we review 'aboveground risks'— political, social, and stakeholder issues. We have a large cohort of experienced international people to evaluate and design company-specific responses. We also use a couple of consulting firms that advise on country, political, and military risks." Having a high profile in the company's home country, "does impact risk management," he says. "We have a good reputation and a retail business, too. We work hard to make sure people realize we intend to live up to our reputation."

It is desirable for a company to update its risk assessment regularly and to understand evolving fraud risks and the specific vulnerabilities that may apply to the company over time. It is common to update risk assessments annually, but in times of significant organizational change or economic volatility more frequent updates may be appropriate.

Risks change and may be evaluated differently when a risk assessment is updated. The application of the Foreign Corrupt Practices Act, for example, has evolved over the past few years from a law that was infrequently enforced and then only with modest penalties into the basis for numerous pending investigations and significant prosecutions with dramatically greater penalties. Globalization has increased the likelihood of encountering bribery and corruption risks while more aggressive prosecutions have increased the consequences. This is a combination with potentially significant impact on a company's risk management needs in this area.

A detailed fraud and corruption risk assessment identifies what types of fraud and corruption a company is most susceptible to, where inside or outside the company it could occur, and how it might be perpetrated.

A fraud and corruption risk assessment can be rendered, less effective when risks are identified only very broadly, failing to be specific in terms of the precise scheme, the part of the company in which it might take place, and which job levels and functions might be involved. For example, the impact of a single sales representative fabricating sales contracts to meet her quota is likely to be radically different from that of the CFO doing the same thing to meet Wall Street's expectations for the company as a whole. And the fraud controls needed to mitigate these risks are quite different. So, being quite specific in identifying fraud schemes and the levels as well as roles of those potentially involved is normally vital.

Risks may vary by country of operations as well. U.S. companies might consider some payments to foreign government officials not to be a risk issue because of the exemption for small "facilitation payments" in the Foreign Corrupt Practices Act. But as Jorge Garcia Villalobos, Forensic and Dispute Services practice leader for Deloitte Mexico, explains, "Here in Mexico everything is a bribe, even from one penny. There is no exemption for a facilitation payment and you need to record it accurately on the books." So something that may not seem like a fraud and corruption risk under U.S. law can be an issue for the company under the laws of another country.

The identified fraud and corruption risks can then be prioritized based on their significance and likelihood. After that, each identified risk can be linked to specific internal controls that reduce the risk of that fraud scheme taking place. Often there will be multiple controls that each partially reduce or mitigate the risk of a particular fraud or corruption risk occurring. The extent of the total risk reduction can be assessed, leading to determination of the residual risk.

If the overall level of residual fraud and corruption risk is greater than the company's risk tolerance (as defined by management and approved by the board of directors), then the company will need to take action to reduce the risk to a tolerable level. This could be a combination of business decisions to avoid certain opportunities that bring excessive risks. It could also be actions to strengthen the fraud controls focused on particular risks, including proactive internal auditing aimed at detecting fraud and corruption schemes.

Fraud and corruption risk assessment overview

Figure 5.1 presents an overview of the fraud and corruption risk assessment process that we suggest.

In our experience, this level of detail benefits the company by fostering risk intelligence—an informed, balanced, and dynamic approach to risk management.

	Step	Approach	Output
1.	Identify and Evaluate Fraud Risk Factors	Identify fraud risk factors	Schedule of fraud risk factors Sound knowledge of fraud risk environment
2.	Identify Possible Fraud Schemes and Scenarios	Identify fraud risks Identify specific fraud schemes Identify account balances and potential errors related to each fraud risk	Pervasive and specific fraud risks Catalog of fraud schemes
3.	Analyze Fraud Risks and Evaluate Control Design and Implementation	Analyze the likelihood and significance of possible fraud schemes Link fraud schemes to mitigating controls and evaluate control design	Inherent risk rating (IRR) of entity Catalog of existing controls Fraud control risk rating Fraud risk related control gap analysis
4.	Evaluate Fraud Risk Assessment Results and Prioritize Residual Fraud Risks	Evaluate the results of fraud risk analysis against established criteria and prioritize risks for treatment	Residual risk rating (RRR) Identification of fraud risks requiring further treatment Fraud risks prioritized
5.	Risk Treatment	Prepare fraud risk action plan Implement plan	Fraud risk action plan Fraud risks treated

Figure 5.1   Sample Fraud Risk Assessment Overview

Opportunities for performance improvement in the area of fraud and corruption risk assessment can often include:

- Linking identified fraud and corruption risks and schemes to specific relevant control activities
- Involving personnel at all levels
- Focusing more on the risk of management override of internal controls
- Conducting assessments for key business units and key countries
- Performing detailed assessments at the fraud and corruption scheme level

Implementing fraud and corruption risk assessments

The fraud and corruption risk assessment is a critical step in addressing fraud and corruption risks within a company and as such would desirably be an area of significant focus for management. However, there is no one standard method by which management may implement its risk assessment. The sample overview shown above is one of several approaches that can be used to assess fraud and corruption risks.

The following generalized implementation plan summarizes elements of a fraud and corruption risk assessment process. It is also a useful guide for developing a practical fraud and corruption risk assessment plan.

In the steps below, we have referred simply to fraud but this should be interpreted broadly to include corruption.

Step One: Identify and Evaluate Fraud and Corruption Risk Factors

As we illustrate in Figure 5.2, fraud risk factors are those events or conditions that indicate:

- Incentives/pressures to perpetrate fraud and corruption,
- Opportunities to carry out the fraud or corruption, or
- Attitudes/rationalizations to justify such an action.

Fraud risk factors do not necessarily indicate the existence of fraud or corruption; however, they often are present in circumstances where fraud or corruption exists.

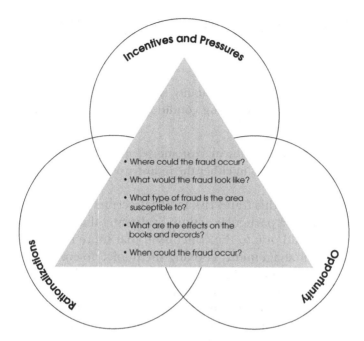

Figure 5.2   Three Categories of Risk Factors

Fraud risk factors are also sometimes referred to as "fraud risk indicators." They mean the same thing. In general, the more fraud risk factors that are present, the greater the level of fraud risk is likely to be overall, although there is not necessarily direct correlation.

Many examples of fraud risk factors are listed in the appendix to U.S. Auditing Standards AU316, *Consideration of Fraud in a Financial Statement Audit*. It is not and cannot be a complete list, but the examples can help to spur thought. In our experience, when people reflect upon some fraud risk factors, others often come to mind, helping to build a more extensive and more nuanced picture of the risk environment. We have included this list of fraud risk factors as an appendix to this book. We encourage you to look it over and consider which ones might apply to your company.

Some fraud risk factors might point to a risk of fraud in a particular area while others are more general. For example, one potential fraud risk factor is:

> Financial stability or profitability is threatened by economic, industry, or entity operating conditions, such as (or indicated by):
>
> - Significant declines in customer demand and increasing business failures in either the industry or overall economy.

As you can see, this fraud risk factor describes a condition, a situation, rather than a particular action. Evaluating this fraud risk factor further might lead one to the conclusion that there is a risk of fraud in the form of management "cooking the books" to conceal financial difficulties. That is a fraud risk, described in general terms. The particular fraud scheme or schemes that could be used to do this would likely depend in part on the specific financial targets that have been set, since sales revenues could be manipulated in a number of ways and profitability generally could be manipulated in additional ways.

It is common for a company to have many fraud risk factors present. Just as Thai food can range from mild through normal to spicy and super-spicy, so, too can fraud risk factors vary in severity. That can also be taken into consideration when fraud risk factors are evaluated, both individually and collectively.

Ideally, personnel from different functions and levels of the company—including management, internal audit, business process owners, IT management, legal, HR, risk/compliance, and fraud/security—would be involved in the fraud and corruption risk assessment process. The audit committee would desirably take an active role in the oversight of management's efforts to identify and consider fraud risk factors as part of the risk assessment process.

Fraud risk factors can be identified through several different means, including interviews, brainstorming sessions, internal and online research and analysis of reports prepared by management, or the internal audit function. Some of these may already be used by management in their consideration of internal controls. For example, if management has elected to assess the control environment through an anonymous survey, the results could also be used to evaluate the existence of fraud risk factors.

Other ways of identifying fraud risk factors include studying past frauds and allegations of fraud in the company, frauds in the industry, unusual financial trends or relationships identified from analytical procedures, and the potential role weak IT controls could play in enabling fraudulent activity to occur.

For companies with more than one operating unit, the process would desirably consider fraud risk factors at the entity level as well as in significant operating units or segments.

Step Two: Identify Possible Fraud and Corruption Risks, Schemes and Accounts Affected

This step involves both the systematic collection of knowledge about fraud schemes and brainstorming about possible fraud schemes and scenarios that could result from the identified fraud risk factors. For example, if a company may find it difficult to comply with certain financial ratios in loan covenants, the brainstorming would desirably include the identification and consideration of scenarios and fraud schemes that could be perpetrated to manipulate those ratios.

This process desirably involves personnel from different functions and levels in the company, including management, internal audit, business process owners, IT management, legal, HR, risk/compliance and fraud/security, with oversight from the audit committee.

Consideration can be given to past frauds and allegations of fraud within the company and the industry. Media searches and databases of reported and alleged frauds can be helpful in identifying fraud risks that could impact the company in the future.

As with investment returns, past experience is not necessarily an accurate predictor of future experience. Organized criminal groups experiment with fraud schemes to identify those with the most promise. Then they exploit them, potentially on a much bigger scale, which can cause fraud losses to increase suddenly for the companies targeted.

The identification of possible fraud and corruption risks would desirably be performed without consideration of the existence or effectiveness of internal controls. This can be a tough exercise, getting to the "inherent risk" in the company, but separating the assessment of fraud and corruption risks from the assessment of the risk mitigation impact of controls, which follows later, helps to produce a higher quality risk assessment.

Where possible, it is desirable to identify the financial statement accounts, the line items, that would be affected by each fraud scheme. That can help make the fraud risk descriptions more precise and can help to integrate the company's consideration of fraud risks for operating and for Sarbanes-Oxley purposes.

Considering the Risk of "Management Override."   Special consideration should be given to the risk of override of controls by management to perpetrate fraud. A 1999 study, *Fraudulent Financial Reporting: 1987–1997*, sponsored by the Committee of Sponsoring Organizations of the Treadway Commission ("COSO"), found that of approximately 200 financial statement frauds at SEC-registered companies between 1987 and 1997, either the CEO or the CFO was involved 83% of the time. Audit committees and boards of directors would be wise to bear this in mind and encourage management to address this risk robustly in the fraud risk assessment.

Management override can also be perpetrated by mid-level managers, exposing the company and senior management to significant risks. It is in the interests of CEOs and CFOs to have strong measures to detect management override taking place.

Our colleague, Jorge Garcia Villalobos, provides another example that demonstrates the value of understanding country-specific customs and practices when preparing a risk assessment and considering the risk of management override. He says that in Mexico, "We have seen that excess trust in local company personnel combined with lack of close supervision and control of subsidiaries by corporate headquarters can result in serious frauds. Local employees may try to show very good results in order to be awarded extra benefits such as bonuses. To accomplish this, they may have a double accounting system, i.e., two sets of books; the real ones and the ones they use to report to corporate headquarters." Mexico is not the only place where that practice takes place, but understanding that it may be more common there could well change the fraud risk assessment.

Staff preparing a company's risk assessment may demonstrate a reluctance to suggest that their CEO, CFO or other senior managers might intentionally "cook the books." When the risk is quietly forgotten or is addressed in a scanty manner, senior executives need to push back and the board or audit committee has the overall responsibility to get that specific risk treated robustly. The staff's position might be unenviable, but the desire to avoid potential conflict cannot be allowed to result in a weak or ineffective fraud risk assessment.

U.S. Auditing Standards AU316 provides examples of ways in which frauds have been committed by management override of existing controls. These examples are:

> (a) recording fictitious journal entries, particularly those recorded close to the end of an accounting period to manipulate operating results, (b) intentionally biasing assumptions and judgments used to estimate account balances, and (c) altering records and terms related to significant and unusual transactions.

Step Three: Assess Identified Fraud and Corruption Risks

This step involves the evaluation of identified fraud and corruption risks and includes the consideration of the following:

Type — The type of risk (i.e., a misappropriation of assets, fraudulent financial reporting, etc.)

Likelihood — The likelihood of the risk occurring. This might be expressed using a simple scale of High, Medium and Low, or using a scale designed to support assessments for Sarbanes-Oxley purposes, such as Remote, Reasonably Possible, and Probable.

Significance — The significance of the risk. For example, is it of a magnitude that could result in a material loss to the company or a material misstatement of the financial statements? As with likelihood, this might be expressed using a simple scale of High, Medium and Low, or using a scale designed to support assessments for Sarbanes-Oxley purposes, such as Inconsequential, More Than Inconsequential, and Material.

Pervasiveness — The pervasiveness of the risk (i.e., whether the potential risk is pervasive to the financial statements as a whole or specifically related to a particular assertion, account, or class of transactions).

With numerous potential fraud and corruption risks often identified, prioritization becomes essential so that focus can be placed on dealing with those risks that present the greatest threat to the company. Emphasis can then be given to those risks considered to be likely, significant, and/or pervasive.

Step Four: Evaluate Mitigating Impact of Controls

Having identified the potentially significant fraud and corruption risks to which the company is exposed, the next step is to evaluate the extent to which controls already in place mitigate the fraud risk.

It is really important to bear in mind at this point that mitigating risk means reducing that risk, not making it totally go away. If only it were that easy! People often seem to think that if you have enough controls the risk goes away and you don't have to worry. In reality, the risk is usually still there, just reduced to a lower level that is desirably within the company's "risk tolerance" set by management with approval of the board of directors.

So when it comes to evaluating the controls a company has to mitigate fraud and corruption risk, the key question is to what extent those controls reduce the risk. If your fraud and corruption risk assessment identifies a number of risks, then sets out a laundry list of controls and assumes that's enough to deal with the problem, there's a further step to take by making an assessment of the extent to which each risk is mitigated. You almost certainly have some fraud or corruption risk remaining, the so-called "residual risk," and it is really valuable to see what that is, as we shall see below.

Another common trap in evaluating the extent to which controls mitigate fraud and corruption risks is grouping all the risks together and then grouping all the controls together and making an overall assessment of whether the group of controls collectively reduces the group of risks to a tolerable level. Such bundling may conceal myriad problems.

The assessment would desirably be made separately for each fraud or corruption risk identified, linking or mapping it to the controls that will help to reduce that risk. This group of controls will typically include both *entity-level* controls that affect the company's entire control environment and *process-level* controls that impact a particular process within a company, such as accounts payable.

In our experience, when each risk is mapped to the specific controls that mitigate that risk, more fraud and corruption risks may be revealed to be under-controlled. Controls may also be listed that would not in practice mitigate the particular risk. For example, requiring two authorized signatures on a journal entry before it is permitted to be processed in the accounting system might help to foil a junior clerk's attempt to cook the books with a bogus accounting entry, but is unlikely to be as effective if the CFO orders the entry to be booked.

A comparison of fraud and corruption risks and controls may also reveal some risks that are over controlled, with duplicative or excessive controls that could be reduced. That scenario is not as common as the under controlling of risks, but it can help to identify control rationalization opportunities, potentially freeing up resources to be redeployed to help protect against more significant risks.

Where controls are not already present, management should consider the need to design and implement additional anti-fraud controls to specifically address the identified fraud and corruption risks. More commonly, the issue is the need to implement control improvements to better mitigate certain fraud and corruption risks that have been revealed to be under-controlled, leaving residual risk in excess of the company's risk tolerance.

Step Five: Evaluate Results & Prioritize Residual Fraud and Corruption Risks for Treatment

Now you have identified your fraud and corruption risks and evaluated the extent to which your fraud controls mitigate each of these risks, you can see your residual risks. You can then compare these with your company's risk tolerance, which ideally has been established by the board of directors.

If you have fraud and corruption risks that exceed your company's risk tolerance, you may have several options to bring them into line:

- Exit the line of business or location that gives rise to that risk. Sometimes that is the best solution for the worst risks.
- Re-organize your business process to reduce the opportunity for that fraud and corruption risk to arise, or to reduce its potential impact. Centralizing cash collections is one example. Sometimes business objectives permit it, sometimes they do not. But look for the opportunity in case it is there.
- Explore ways to transfer that risk, through outsourcing, changing contract terms with suppliers/customers, or insurance.
- Add or strengthen controls focused on that fraud or corruption risk.

Note that we put strengthening controls last. Make no mistake, we love strong fraud controls. We just do not believe in adding more controls if there is a better solution. It is worth considering other options before you conclude more controls are needed.

Risk assessment reports: the good, the bad, and the invisible

Fraud and corruption risk assessments necessarily consider many different risk factors, risks, specific schemes, and potential perpetrators. Keeping all of that organized usually requires a spreadsheet or a database.

A good fraud and corruption risk assessment template can help drive quality and consistency across a company as different business units identify and assess their fraud risks. Consistency becomes very important when you come to consolidate those risk assessments and produce a summary for senior management, the board of directors, or the audit committee.

The guidance paper, *Managing the Business Risk of Fraud: A Practical Guide,* has an example of a fraud risk assessment framework as an exhibit. It's a good starting point, though some more sophisticated companies may want to add some extra features. Figure 5.3 is our variation on this theme and adds a place to identify relevant fraud risk factors, as well as separating the descriptions of fraud and corruption risks and their specific schemes, to help drive the specificity that can be lacking in practice.

If your company's fraud risk assessment contains these features, you have a good chance of producing a useful end product.

Spreadsheets and databases are great for the people who need the details, such as the managers responsible for fraud and corruption risks within their business units, or for the internal auditors who monitor management's fraud risk and controls assessments. But they can easily become overwhelming for senior executives, board members, and audit committees, especially if they become voluminous. A one page summary of the top-ten fraud and corruption risks might be more effective with this audience than a 100-page detailed spreadsheet.

Fraud Risk Factors	Fraud Risk	Fraud Scheme	Account Affected	Potential Parties Involved	Likelihood	Significance	Inherent Risk Rating	Control Activities	Control Effectiveness	Residual Risk	Risk Treatment
High degree of competition Decline in customer demand Earnings expectation of analysts Significant incentive compensation for management	Financial statement fraud – overstate revenue	Fictitious sales to phony customers	Sales and accounts receivable	Sales managers	Reasonably possible	High	High	Code of conduct Ethics training Whistle-blower hotline Review of major or unusual sales by sales VPs	Effective	Medium	Internal audit to perform analytical review and data mining to identify potential fraud

Figure 5.3   Example of Fraud Risk Assessment Framework

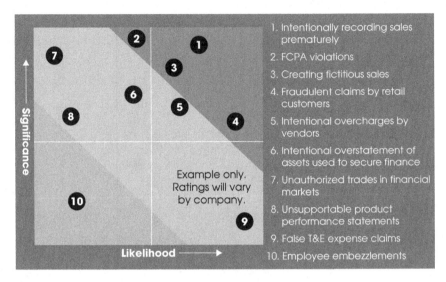

Figure 5.4   Heat Map of Fraud and Corruption Risks

A "heat map" is a great tool to help you visualize what's important. Internal auditors and other risk assessment professionals use these and they can work well for fraud and corruption risks too – if you use them right.

Let's revisit the heat map of fraud and corruption risks we introduced earlier in the book. A heat map shows the likelihood of specific types of fraud and corruption risks and the potential significance of the each risk's impact.

The sample heat map in Figure 5.4 shows the hypothetical results of a fraud and corruption risk assessment for one company with ten risks identified. It is simplified since in reality there would often be many risks identified that were not considered significant, cluttering up the bottom half of the chart.

The top right corner of the heat map is normally shaded hot red, identifying fraud and corruption risks that have high likelihood of occurring and high potential significance. These usually get everyone's attention, and rightly so.

The bottom-left corner of the heat map is normally shaded cool green, identifying fraud and corruption risks with low likelihood of occurring and low potential significance even if they do arise. These usually get little attention, and that's generally fine as long as they are accurately assessed.

The band across the heat map sweeping from the top-left corner to the bottom-right corner is normally shaded warm orange. This contains fraud and corruption risks that have high significance but low likelihood (top left) or high likelihood but low significance (bottom right).

High-likelihood but low-significance fraud and corruption risks might include thefts of office supplies or small travel and expense claim frauds. They are unlikely to break the company. But high-significance and low-likelihood fraud and corruption risks are different. They *can* break the company. These often include financial statement fraud perpetrated by senior managers or executives— unlikely but potentially devastating both financially and in terms of the reputation of the company.

It would be a mistake to focus solely on the red section of the heat map and the fraud and corruption risks in the top right quadrant, giving insufficient attention to the potentially catastrophic risks lurking in the top left quadrant. *The nasty surprises that lead to major corporate frauds might be better prevented or sooner detected if management, boards of directors and audit committees scrutinized the items in that top left quadrant skeptically.*

Four quadrants; four risk management strategies

As we just discussed, a fraud and corruption risk heat map has four quadrants, representing the four different possible combinations of high and low likelihood and high and low potential significance. Each fraud or corruption risk will fall into just one quadrant.

As you look at your fraud and corruption risk heat map and consider how best to manage your company's fraud and corruption risks, an overarching strategy is good. But in reality you'll likely want to deal with the risks in those four quadrants in four different ways.

Imagine Figure 5.5 superimposed over the fraud and corruption risk heat map. Each of the four images characterizes the types of fraud and corruption risks associated with each of the four quadrants of the heat map.

The bottom left quadrant we call the "fleas quadrant." These are fraud and corruption risks with low likelihood of occurring and low significance even if they do occur. Normally you wouldn't invest

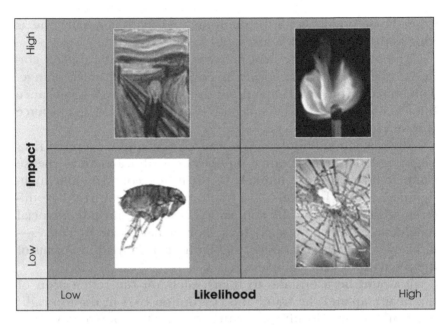

Figure 5.5 Four Types of Fraud and Corruption Risks

Fears ("The Scream") image: ©2008 The Munch Museum/The Munch-Ellingsen Group/Artists Rights Society (ARS), NY; Fleas image: ©iStockphoto.com/Oliver Sun Kim; Fires (match flame) image: ©iStockphoto.com/Sille Van Landschoot; Flaws (broken window) image: ©iStockphoto.com/David H. Lewis.

much time and effort to prevent them, but if you do discover them then it is time for appropriate punitive action.

The bottom right quadrant we call the "flaws quadrant." These are fraud and corruption risks with high likelihood of occurring but relatively low significance. Fraudulent travel and entertainment expense claims are a common example. Frauds of this type exploit imperfections in business processes that may be tolerable to the company from a cost-benefit perspective, but which can permit relatively small frauds to arise.

Computer-assisted internal audit techniques and continuous monitoring systems can help to detect these kinds of frauds efficiently. Once flagged, they can be investigated and resolved. But the primary goal would desirably be to identify ways to strengthen the core business process and refine controls across the company as a whole to keep the cost of these frauds down. Individually, they are small, so the investigation costs can best be justified by the value of the additional frauds prevented through the process improvements made.

The top-right quadrant we call the "fires quadrant." These are fraud and corruption risks that have a high likelihood of occurring and that have high potential significance to the company. For a credit card issuer, these might be credit card frauds by customers and organized criminal groups. For an insurer, claims fraud. For a banker, loan fraud. If you do not manage these types of risks aggressively, you could be out of business, or at least severely less profitable, quickly.

Aggressive investment in anti-fraud personnel, processes, and technology to prevent, deter, and detect these kinds of frauds can yield returns on investment (ROI) that can easily be several hundred or even several thousand percent in industry segments with raging fraud "fires." Measure the ROI carefully and then continue to invest aggressively until the ROI falls to match what you make by selling your products or services. Anti-fraud chiefs in these industries often make their CFO's smile with the ROI they achieve. And their CFO's are often happy to invest more.

We have saved the best, and most important, quadrant for last. We call the top left quadrant the "fears quadrant," and it is represented in Figure 5.5 by Edvard Munch's famous picture, "The Scream". This quadrant contains fraud and corruption risks that have a relatively low likelihood of occurring, but have high potential significance, either financially or in terms of reputation. As stated above, cooking the books by senior management is a classic example.

Historically, companies may have put some general antifraud controls in place (a code of conduct, ethics training and maybe a whistle-blower hotline) and felt that was either sufficient or the best they could do to address these unlikely risks. We see that changing.

Companies need not view these fraud and corruption risks as unpredictable lightning strikes that cannot be managed. Just as Doppler weather radar can warn airplane pilots of microburst conditions that could be fatal upon takeoff or landing, so too can people, processes and technology be deployed to better protect companies from low-likelihood high-significance fraud and corruption risks.

In the "fires quadrant," we discussed using ROI as a measure and pursuing profit enhancement. In the fears quadrant the name of the game is risk management. Based on its risk tolerance, the company can look for indications that some of its most-feared fraud and corruption risks may actually be occurring in practice.

Monitoring and detection tools can be programmed to search accounting systems for signs of potential bribery and corruption.

Different financial statement fraud schemes can be tested for using computerized tools. You don't expect to find these major frauds taking place, but you look to some extent, nevertheless, to help prevent and deter them and to detect them more quickly if they do occur.

This is an area where we see a great opportunity for change in fraud risk management practices. It is one where we think audit committees, boards of directors, and senior executives will come to confront their fears and will find that fraud and corruption risks can be better managed by doing so.

Questions to ask about your fraud and corruption risk assessment

Asking the following questions can help you identify potential opportunities to enhance your company's fraud and corruption risk assessment:

1. Does your company have formal and regularly scheduled procedures to perform fraud and corruption risk assessments?
2. Are appropriate personnel involved in your fraud and corruption risk assessment?
3. Are fraud and corruption risk assessments performed at all appropriate levels of the company (such as the entity level, significant locations or business units, significant account balance, or major process level)?
4. Does your fraud and corruption risk assessment include consideration of internal and external risk factors (including pressures or incentives, rationalizations or attitudes, and opportunities)?
5. Does your fraud and corruption risk assessment include the identification and evaluation of past occurrences and allegations of fraud and corruption within the entity and industry? Does it include the evaluations of unusual financial trends or relationships identified from analytical procedures or techniques?
6. Does your fraud and corruption risk assessment consider the risk of management's override of controls?
7. Does management consider the type, likelihood, significance, and pervasiveness of identified fraud and corruption risks?

8. Is your fraud and corruption risk assessment updated periodically to include considerations of changes in operations, new information systems, acquisitions, changes in job roles and responsibilities, employees in new positions, results from self-assessments of controls, monitoring activities, internal audit findings, new or evolving industry trends, and revisions to identified fraud and corruption risks within the company?
9. Does management assess the design and operating effectiveness of the fraud and corruption risk assessment process?
10. Does management adequately document its assessments and conclusions regarding the design and operating effectiveness of the fraud and corruption risk assessment process?

Real World Example

Even though a company had been performing a fraud risk assessment in the past, it did not consider how it was vulnerable to specific fraud schemes. After performing a detailed fraud risk assessment, the company identified exposure to collusive fraud, one where employees colluded with outside parties, in its treasury function that was unmitigated by any controls. As a result, the company instituted an additional control for treasury disbursements that identified a collusive cash defalcation scheme, that had been occurring and had gone undetected for some time. Making its fraud risk assessment more detailed by considering fraud schemes and mitigating controls helped this company to identify the fraud and to minimize future financial losses.

CHAPTER 6

Company-wide Anti-Fraud Controls: The Role of the Control Environment and High-Level Strategies

Key points:

➢ Corporate wide strategies are an important element of setting a fraud and corruption risk management strategy.

➢ Such strategies emphasize the importance of the fraud and corruption risk assessment process reviewed in the previous chapter.

➢ A key element of company-wide strategies is the control environment.

➢ Components of the control environment function to mitigate risks identified in the fraud and corruption risk assessment.

➢ A control environment is not scheme-specific – it is company-specific.

➢ The importance of a company's control environment is widely recognized by issuers of anti-fraud and anti-corruption guidance.

➢ A company's control environment is an important element of both its anti-fraud and anti-corruption strategies.

Creating an anti-fraud control environment

In this chapter we discuss the primary importance of establishing a strong control environment. As we will demonstrate, the control environment is a crucial element of anti-fraud and anti-corruption strategies. Like a well-built barn that protects the crops or livestock in it from the storms that periodically rage outside, it is a vital piece of equipment. Without its protection, activities could be disrupted and assets destroyed every time a storm came along.

Make no mistake. The control environment is not window dressing, nor can it be an afterthought. It is absolutely essential.

What exactly is a *control environment* and why is it important?

A strong control environment sets an appropriate tone for the company's attitude toward unethical behavior, including fraud. It's not a loose collection of touchy-feely management aphorisms. A strong control environment:

- Fosters a culture of honesty
- Promotes ethical behavior
- Provides discipline for violations of the code of ethics/conduct
- Sets an appropriate tone for the entity's attitudes toward fraud and fraud prevention
- Promotes controls to prevent, deter, and detect fraud

The control environment usually includes, among other items, a clearly written code of ethics and conduct, a confidential reporting mechanism such as a whistle-blower hotline or helpline, suitable employee training, and a system for responding meaningfully when control deficiencies are pointed out and allegations of fraud are raised.

Just as the barn creates a protective space in which the farmer can operate effectively whatever the weather, so a strong control environment creates a workplace where business can be conducted, sheltered from some of the potential risks of fraud and corruption.

The control environment can be supplemented with specific anti-fraud and anti-corruption activities as well, just as a barn can benefit from an alert farm cat to keep the mice and rats at bay.

Other anti-fraud activities operate inside the environment, such as controls targeting various forms of fraud and corruption, as well as strategies designed to investigate and respond to crises.

Tone at the top

A key element of the control environment is the "tone at the top" of a company. Every company has one, intentionally or otherwise. The question is whether that tone fosters ethical behavior or whether it seems to tolerate lapses in ethical behavior in favor of a focus on short-term financial results. The words and actions of senior executives are a critical part of the tone at the top. Senior executives set the tone and put in place the other elements of the control environment to deliver their message across the company.

"Senior executives need to set the tone because their reputations are at stake," says Dr. Olivier Brasseur, director of the Division for Oversight Services at the United Nations Population Fund. "Senior executives need to understand that when their reputations are damaged, they also lose their credibility and their authority to lead."

Warren Buffett is a good example of a top executive who sets high ethical standards for his employees. In testimony before Congress, when he took the helm as chairman and chief executive of embattled Salomon Brothers, he said:

> I want employees to ask themselves whether they are willing to have any contemplated act appear on the front page of their local paper the next day, be read by their spouses, children, and friends ... If they follow this test, they will not fear my other message to them: Lose money for my firm and I will be understanding; lose a shred of reputation for the firm, and I will be ruthless.

While the tone of the control environment flows from the top, everyone in the company is responsible for its success. To put it more bluntly, everyone needs to be on board and actively participating.

For example, the audit committee can be actively involved in the oversight of management's efforts to create and deploy anti-fraud controls, and can encourage management to confirm not only that fraud risks are pinpointed but that control activities are established and carried out. The internal audit function in most companies also has a critical role in making sure that anti-fraud processes are implemented and working properly.

Public Company Accounting Oversight Board Auditing Standard No. 5, issued July 12, 2007, puts the broad concept of the control environment into sharp focus by noting the responsibility of external auditors to judge the effectiveness of the control environment at SEC registrants that are subject to certain reporting requirements:

> Because of its importance to effective internal control over financial reporting, the auditor must evaluate the control environment at the company. As part of evaluating the control environment, the auditor should assess:
> - Whether management's philosophy and operating style promote effective internal control over financial reporting
> - Whether sound integrity and ethical values, particularly of top management, are developed and understood and
> - Whether the Board or audit committee understands and exercises oversight responsibility over financial reporting and internal control.

The COSO internal controls framework, developed by the Committee of Sponsoring Organization of the Treadway Commission ("COSO"), is used by many companies as the framework for their internal control structure. The control environment is a key component of the COSO framework. Establishing a control environment is critical to the success of a company-wide anti-fraud strategy since it creates and sustains a culture that embraces honesty and rejects fraud.

The control environment as a bulwark

As we have made clear throughout this book, preventing fraud completely is not a realistic objective. It is, however, possible to put measures in place that would prevent and discourage some frauds from occurring, and detect many of those that do occur, focusing on preventing and detecting significant frauds.

A strong control environment enhances a fraud risk management program's effectiveness. In a sense it is diffuse, desirably covering an entire company. Among other things, it should desirably cause employees, customers, and others who may be contemplating frauds, or could be, to pause and consider. It is meant to cause people to think about the right thing to do. Unlike more narrowly focused controls, like those discussed in the next two chapters, its function is to be generally preventive.

The control environment can involve many possible dimensions and encompass multiple elements, ranging from very high-level considerations such as the statements of directors and company management to the effect that fraud and corruption will not be tolerated, to more particular mechanisms such as compensation schemes meant to encourage honesty and transparency in formulating and reporting results.

The control environment also can entail recruiting practices designed to identify candidate employees with desired versus undesired psychological or behavioral attributes and the development and propagation of ethics programs designed to encourage appropriate employee decision making.

By providing discipline, structure, and motivation, the control environment serves as the foundation for all the various processes that prevent, deter, and detect fraud. In a resilient corporation, the control environment is pervasive. It is ingrained deeply into every aspect of the company.

The control environment and governance

Effective governance processes are foundational elements of a company's fraud risk management strategy. The audit committee, typically a committee of the board of directors, has responsibility for some parts of governance, for monitoring the financial reporting process, for overseeing the internal control system and anti-fraud programs and controls, and for overseeing the internal audit and independent public accountant.

The audit committee is also responsible for reporting its findings to the board of directors. In general, it is desirable for those charged with governance to have a reasonable basis for believing that management implements policies encouraging ethical behavior; monitor the company's fraud risk management effectiveness; and appoint at least one executive-level member of management to be responsible for coordinating fraud risk management and reporting to the board on the topic.

Put it in writing

As part of the company's governance structure, a fraud risk management program would desirably be in place, including a written policy to convey the expectations of the board of directors, the audit committee, and executive management to assess and manage fraud risk.

There are several formats for written policies, including variations of the options listed below:

- A single comprehensive and complete document addressing all aspects of fraud control.
- A brief strategy outline emphasizing the attributes of fraud control, but leaving the design to each of the business units.
- An outline referencing relevant policies.

Elements of an effective strategy usually include:

- Full commitment of the Board and company
- Fraud awareness training
- Roles and responsibilities of various functions and levels in fraud risk management
- Conflict of interest disclosure processes
- Periodic affirmation processes
- Fraud risk assessment and control planning
- Reporting procedures
- Investigation, discipline and prosecution guidance
- Corrective action, where appropriate
- Fraud risk management process monitoring, evaluation and improvement

An outline of a practical fraud and corruption control strategy can be found in *Australian Standard 8001-2008 Fraud and Corruption Control*, published in 2008 by Standards Australia.

Setting the tone

At the beginning of this chapter we touched on the central importance of the tone at the top, which sets the standard for behavior across the company. Senior management, the board of directors, and the audit committee have the primary responsibility of creating the tone.

It is also crucial to remember that the company's tone at the top extends beyond traditional boundaries by setting standards for business partners, agents, investors, customers, suppliers – the company's entire extended value chain.

So, what is this tone at the top and how does a company create an appropriate one? Let's begin by looking at two key characteristics of a good tone at the top.

1. The company has a culture and a work environment that promotes open communication, consultation and ethical behavior.
2. The senior executives walk the talk and lead by example when it comes to ethical behavior.

What are the key determinants of ethical behavior? They include company variables as well as variables at work outside the company: the behavior of superiors, the behavior of peers, formal policies of the company, industry-wide ethical standards and practices, and, of course, the prevailing moral climate of society at large.

Good tone at the top reduces the chances of employees committing fraud by clearly communicating a zero-tolerance attitude toward any and all fraud. Effective tone at the top unambiguously rejects fraud and corruption as acceptable business practices. When senior management sends clear, unambiguous messages stating its unalterable opposition to fraud and corruption at every level and for any reason, these messages can override potentially negative influences that might tempt some people to commit wrongful acts.

A strong and unambiguous tone at the top is also likely to result in a more favorable work environment that attracts better job candidates, encourages employee retention and reduces unnecessary turnover, leading to a more stable and generally more motivated workforce.

There are many ways for management to set the right tone, but some of the simplest are straightforward:

1. Communicate what is expected of employees.
2. Lead by example.
3. Provide a safe mechanism for reporting violations.
4. Reward integrity.

Internal audit's role

Internal audit also has a role in supporting senior management's efforts to set the right tone for the company. It helps by testing controls, such as those requiring employees to acknowledge that they have received and read the company's code of conduct and ethics. Internal audit can evaluate how employees perceive and understand the tone at the top. Internal audit, along with the company's legal function and human resources function, can also play a role in following up on allegations of employee conduct violations when they are reported through the whistle-blower hotline or other channels.

Mike Novosel, chief audit executive at Chicago-based True Value Company, puts it this way,

> There are numerous fraud risks that you just can't mitigate. You can have all the controls in the world, but if two or three people get together and decide to circumvent around a control, there's not much you can do to stop them. So the most important preventive controls are 'soft controls' such as hiring the right people and setting the right tone at the top.

We are calling attention to the particular duties of internal audit to underscore the notion that responsibility for establishing, maintaining and communicating tone at the top across the company falls on many shoulders. Good "tone at the top" isn't just a responsibility of senior executives – in a very real sense, it's the responsibility of everyone in the company.

Measuring tone at the top

The phrase, "if you can't measure it, you can't manage it" also applies to "tone at the top." But how do you measure something that seems so, well, diffuse? Well, there are several quite sophisticated ways that are increasingly used for this purpose. Employee feedback, cultural surveys and exit interviews offer excellent opportunities for collecting valuable information about the quality and effectiveness of a company's "tone at the top."

You can also conduct interviews and discussions with employees, hold discussions with the internal audit team, and review management's communications with employees. Since those communications are disseminated across various channels (including email, intranet, and voicemail) that will often provide enough material to develop a detailed picture of how well or how poorly management communicates its moral and ethical policies to the rest of the company, and how well this communication is understood and applied by the broader employee workforce.

Written code of ethics/conduct

One of the most effective mechanisms for promoting ethical behavior is a written code of ethics or code of conduct. Generally speaking, a code of ethics/conduct includes provisions related to conflicts of interest, related-party transactions, illegal acts, and the monitoring of the code by management and the audit committee or board.

Section 406 of the Sarbanes-Oxley Act of 2002 and the SEC's Final Rule, *Disclosure Required by Sections 406 and 407 of the Sarbanes-Oxley Act of 2002,* require a listed company to disclose whether it has adopted a code of ethics and if it has not, to explain why. The NYSE and NASDAQ listing standards require the adoption and public disclosure of a code of business conduct and ethics.

The SEC's final rule defines the term code of ethics as, written standards that are reasonably designed to deter wrongdoing and to promote:

- Honest and ethical conduct, including the ethical handling of actual or apparent conflicts of interest between personal and professional relationships
- Full, fair, accurate, timely, and understandable disclosure in reports and documents that a registrant files with, or submits to, the Commission and in other public communications made by the registrant
- Compliance with applicable governmental laws, rules, and regulations
- Prompt internal reporting to an appropriate person or persons identified in the code of violations of the code
- Accountability for adherence to the code

Why is a code important?

As mentioned above, listed companies are required to disclose whether they have adopted a written code, and if they haven't adopted a code, they're required to explain the reasons.

Additionally, the code ideally provides a clear statement of business principles encapsulating the company's value system.

Imagine that for a moment—a single document setting forth the expected cultural norms of an entire company. Such a document has both power and value. Resilient corporations tend to view the creation of a code of ethics/conduct as a process that creates value. They tend to see the code as a strategic asset, and not as a cost of doing business.

So, what's in a code? First, it provides all employees, officers, directors, suppliers, and agents with guidance on acceptable behavior relating to common areas of risk. These might include topics such as:

- Compliance with laws and regulations
- General employee conduct
- Conflicts of interest
- Outside activities, employment, and directorships of employees
- Relationships with clients and suppliers
- Gifts and entertainment
- Favors, kickbacks, or secret commissions
- Entity communications
- Privacy and confidentiality
- Dealing with outside people and entities
- Sexual harassment
- Fraud

Excerpts from Deloitte Code of Ethics and Professional Conduct

An example that's close to our hearts is the *Code of Ethics and Professional Conduct* for our organization, Deloitte Financial Advisory Services LLP. This Deloitte code provides detailed information, guidance, and references to written policies and resources that can help us "make the right choices on a daily basis."

The code explains in detail the responsibilities of all employees, clearly sets the firm's level of expectation, and lists contact information for sources of practical advice on following the code.

In addition to covering basic issues and values, the code unambiguously conveys Deloitte's tone at the top. It asks every employee to consider these questions to aid in making the right decision about a possible course of action:

- Are my actions illegal or unethical?
- Am I being fair and honest?
- Would I be unwilling or embarrassed to tell my family, friends, or co-workers?
- Would the reputation of a Deloitte U.S. entity be harmed if the action were revealed in the newspapers?
- Am I personally uncomfortable about the course of action?
- Could someone's life, health, safety, or reputation be endangered by my action?
- Could the intended action appear inappropriate to a third party?

The code then states, "If you are still unsure of what to do, ask questions and seek additional guidance . . . " The code contains a wealth of contact information, cross-references to detailed guidance and applicable policies, and other useful suggestions for finding the answers to potentially complex questions.

The code is useful and user-friendly. The code prominently promotes integrity as a "core value", and concisely defines integrity as "always trying to do the right thing, the first time, every time."

The code also states in highly visible type, "There will be no reprisals against anyone because he or she, in good faith, reports an ethics or compliance concern."

We can tell you from our own experience that the code is both a useful tool and an indispensable, foundational element of the control environment here at Deloitte.

How does management create a successful code of ethics/conduct?

Any code, no matter how valuable, is likely to encounter resistance if employees feel as though it's been imposed on them. So it's essential to encourage a sense of employee ownership of concept and content when the code is developed.

It is probably not a good idea to write the code at a top-level management retreat. Try to make sure the code is developed in a collaborative environment that encourages input from all levels across the company. Don't work in a vacuum.

The code should be written in a manner that makes it relatively easy to update over time. Flexibility is the key here. The code can be firm, but it shouldn't be rigid.

After the code is written and distributed, it is important to identify and explain the benefits of adhering to it. It is also crucial to demonstrate that management is willing to reward ethical conduct, and punish unethical behavior. Actions that reinforce the integrity of the code should be recognized, and when appropriate, rewarded. Periodically, employees may be required to demonstrate understanding of the code.

Ethics training for all employees—including management

It would be naïve to assume that every employee who reads their company's code of ethics/conduct will walk away with the same understanding. You should consider implementing a formal training regimen that could include testing and periodic refresher courses.

Training reinforces the company's ethical values and anti-fraud control environment. Tailored training based on the company's identified risks, including fraud risks, is likely to be more effective than generic content.

Testing is often part of the training regimen, since you will want a way of proving that employees have actually absorbed the lessons, understand the code of ethics/conduct and know what is expected of them in terms of ethical behavior.

Periodic surveys of the workforce can be valuable, since they will tend to reveal deficiencies or problems in the control environment that could open doors to fraud or other mis-behavior.

An adjunct to ethics training is fraud awareness training. Making employees aware of common schemes and, at least in outline, the steps that the company is taking to avoid or mitigate them can enhance employees' effectiveness in deterring and detecting fraud.

The net takeaway here is that new employees need training, and all employees benefit from periodic refresher training. Training is an essential component of the modern fraud control environment.

Hotlines, helplines and whistle-blower programs

Section 301 of the Sarbanes-Oxley Act of 2002 requires each issuer's audit committee to establish procedures for:

- The receipt, retention, and treatment of complaints received by the issuer regarding accounting, internal accounting controls, or auditing matters
- The confidential, anonymous submission by employees of the issuer of concerns regarding questionable accounting or auditing matters

This requirement is commonly fulfilled by providing a hotline, (or *helpline* as some companies prefer to position it) along with other mechanisms for reporting such as email, Web forms, fax and mail. In addition to making them accessible to employees, consider making them available to individuals outside of the company (i.e., vendors, customers, agents, and even the general public) to report potential fraudulent behavior.

Training will help employees to know how and when to use the hotline. Procedures will be needed for handling complaints and for accepting confidential "whistle-blower" submissions about questionable accounting or auditing matters.

Why are hotlines so important to the control environment? The answer is stark and simple: the most common way in which workplace frauds of all kinds are uncovered is through tips. According to the Association of Certified Fraud Examiners' *2008 Report to the Nation on Occupational Fraud and Abuse,* 46 percent of the nearly 1,000 frauds in their study were detected that way. In public companies the figure was 54 percent and in private companies it was 38 percent. In any case, it is extremely valuable to have a robust system in place for encouraging, enabling and rewarding the reporting of potential wrongdoing.

Employees need to know that they can report their suspicions without fear of retaliation. They need to know that their willingness to use the system when necessary will not result in them losing their jobs or getting entangled in legal proceedings.

In addition to serving as a deterrent for unacceptable behavior, the goal of a hotline is to enable the company to identify and resolve issues early, potentially mitigating liability. It demonstrates management's due diligence, and complies with the Sarbanes-Oxley

Act of 2002 and the Federal Sentencing Guidelines for organizations, which define the elements of an effective compliance and ethics program.

Our colleague David Williams, chief executive officer of Deloitte Financial Advisory Services LLP, says you can learn a lot about the state of a company's control environment simply by looking at its whistle-blower program.

> Some companies would prefer not having a whistle-blower program because they think it will uncover issues they don't really want to deal with. Some companies mostly use their hotlines to put out fires. Other companies see the hotline as a source of valuable information and insight that can help them identify trends and deal with issues before they become potentially dangerous. Those companies see their anti-fraud strategies as investments, not as costs, and they're the ones that tend to be more successful.

We agree with David's premise, and we urge you to ask yourself whether your company regards its hotline as a cost or an asset.

Characteristics of a good whistle-blower program:

- Hotlines or other confidential reporting mechanisms are accessible to all personnel.
- Management should consider making hotlines available to people outside the company – vendors, customers, agents and even the general public.
- Management has made it clear there is zero tolerance for retaliation for good faith reports.
- Training to ensure that all employees know how to use the hotline.
- The adequacy of procedures for handling complaints is assessed.
- A formal program and procedures for proper follow up on reported allegations is implemented.
- Procedures are in place to support the confidentiality of the whistle-blower processes and prevent unauthorized access to data.
- Key metrics of the hotline, such as call volume, are regularly benchmarked against industry standards.

- Regular communication to all personnel to advise them the hotline is an available resource.
- Anonymous cultural surveys are used to gauge employees' confidence in and understanding of the hotline mechanism.

The role of human resources—employee selection and discipline

Let's be candid. The effectiveness of automated controls to prevent fraud can be overcome. In the real world, many internal control activities still depend largely on the effectiveness and judgment of individuals. The quality of these individuals is a relevant issue for the simple reason that people, not machines, are currently the most effective defense against most fraud and corruption.

Consistent hiring and promotion of high-integrity individuals can be a visible demonstration that management is serious about setting the right tone and maintaining a control environment throughout the company.

The human resources function obviously plays a prominent role in hiring and retaining a high-quality workforce. So it makes sense for companies to ensure that appropriate standards exist for hiring and promoting personnel.

For all employees, particularly senior management and those individuals with influence over financial reporting or who are involved in the preparation of the financial statements (including board of directors, audit committee, general counsel, CFO, and controllers), these standards may include a background investigation confirming prior education, work experience, evidence of integrity, and a search for evidence of criminal activity. Such steps taken should desirably be documented and reviewed by appropriate personnel.

Management may also consider performing background investigations for existing employees being promoted into a position of trust and on a periodic basis for those serving in such positions. Employees who join the company through mergers or acquisitions are also candidates for such checks, especially if comparable procedures were not in place at their former company.

Moreover, the U.S. Sentencing Commission's *Federal Sentencing Guidelines Manual* states that specific individuals within management should be assigned overall responsibility for compliance and ethics. The Commission also recommends that organizations use due care not to delegate substantial discretionary authority to individuals the organization knows, or should have known through the exercise of due diligence, to have engaged in illegal activities or other conduct inconsistent with an effective compliance and ethics program.

Management should also consider periodic communications to employees regarding disciplinary actions the company has taken against employees found to have engaged in unethical and perhaps fraudulent behavior. A corner of the company's employee newsletter (likely an email or intranet page these days) is a great vehicle to do this. The legal and human resources functions would play a key role in qualifying and formulating the messages. Legal counsel would likely require that names and other details that would identify the individuals be omitted.

Opportunities should not be missed to demonstrate to employees that the company takes its values and code of conduct seriously and consistently takes disciplinary action, including termination, where appropriate.

In Chapter 8, we will also take up the question of whether employee psychological or behavioral evaluation makes sense as a detection mechanism.

This is all another way of saying, "know your employees," because you may be held accountable if you have not taken the proper steps to check their backgrounds and assess their integrity.

Other general strategies of which fraud risk management is a component

Before moving on to our chapters about specific preventive and detective controls, let's take a brief look at several other existing strategies for managing fraud risks. We do not believe that any of these strategies would function as a stand-alone solution, but they should be considered as potentially useful components of a comprehensive fraud risk management strategy.

We also note that the strategies, which tend to be cut from whole cloth, and therefore involve concerns that are more varied than managing fraud risk, are very much a part of current management theory discourse.

Enterprise risk management

Risk management and ERM (Enterprise Risk Management) have been familiar terms in the financial services industry for more than a decade. It is only recently that ERM programs have gained wider acceptance beyond the financial services industry.

It appears likely that the financial sector's experience with ERM may be studied carefully by companies that want to do a better job of managing the entire spectrum of risks facing them. Why do we believe this is a particularly good idea at this time? Well, if we have learned anything in the past decade, it is that the most dangerous risks are the ones you do not anticipate and do not prepare for. As we stated earlier, the pace at which new risks emerge seems to be accelerating.

We think that ERM fits closely with the central thesis of this book, that successful companies are the ones that foster resiliency in regard to the risk of fraud and corruption and that do so by focusing on assessing risks, then putting company-wide as well as specific controls in place. Such companies also focus on the need to put in place fraud investigation and other response capabilities.

What exactly is ERM? According to COSO, ERM is "a process affected by an entity's board of directors, management and other personnel, applied in strategy setting and across the enterprise, designed to identify potential events that may affect the entity. ERM provides a framework to manage risk according to the company's appetite and offers reasonable assurance regarding the achievement of its objectives."

The Institute of Internal Auditors defines ERM as "a rigorous and coordinated approach to assess and respond to all risks that affect the achievement of an organization's strategic and financial objectives; includes both upside and downside risks."

Fundamentals of ERM

ERM can take many forms, so it would be useful to list some of its fundamental concepts. Generally speaking, effective ERM is:

- A process, ongoing and flowing through an entity
- Effected by people at every level of a company
- Applied in a strategy setting

- Applied across the enterprise, at every level and unit, and includes taking an entity-level portfolio view of risk
- Designed to identify potential events that, if they occur, will affect the entity and to manage risk within its risk appetite
- Able to provide reasonable assurance to an entity's management and board of directors
- Geared to achievement of objectives in one or more separate but overlapping categories

In addition to aligning risk appetite and strategy, ERM should help the company enhance its risk response decisions, reduce operational surprise and losses, identify and manage multiple and cross-enterprise risks, seize legitimate business opportunities, and improve the deployment of capital.

The goals of an ERM program are quite straightforward. First, the program can facilitate an understanding among the board and senior management of how their company's risks are being managed on a daily basis. The program can also aggregate significant risk information and integrate it through the company to create one view of the enterprise's risk profile and status.

Finally, an effective ERM strategy can have the capability of equipping the various segments of the company with the capacity to consistently identify, evaluate and report on the control of their significant risks, both financial and non-financial.

Achieving risk intelligence

We believe that resilient corporations try to elevate their ERM capabilities to the point at which they are "risk intelligent." Our colleagues who focus on this area like to call these model companies "risk intelligent enterprises." No matter what designation you choose, these corporations are likely to share the following characteristics:

- Their risk management capabilities span the entire company, and are not limited to individual business units or silos.
- Their risk management practices cover a wide spectrum of new and emerging risks, not just obvious ones.
- They disseminate what they learn from their risk management practices across the enterprise so that everyone with an

interest in mitigating risk can share the knowledge that is created by the company's risk management systems.
- They leverage their investments in risk management
technologies and processes to create value for the business.

Among the potential competitive benefits of an effective risk
intelligence strategy are:

- Improved ability to prevent, quickly detect, correct, and escalate critical risk issues
- Reduced burden on business operations by standardizing risk
management principles and language
- Reduced cost of risk management by improved sharing of
risk information and integration of existing risk management
functions
- A means to improve strategic flexibility for both upside and
downside scenarios
- The ability to provide a "comfort level" to the board and other
stakeholders that the full range of risks is understood and
managed

Fundamentals of GRC

Another corporate strategy involving fraud risk management that
has gained traction in recent years is GRC, which stands for *governance, risk* and *compliance.* For the purposes of this discussion, we're
using these definitions:

Governance—culture, policies, organization structure, and
processes by which companies are directed and controlled;
provides the structure through which company objectives
are set, and the means of attaining those objectives and
monitoring performance

Risk—the effect of estimated uncertainty on business objectives;
risk management is the coordinated activity to pursue opportunity while managing adverse events and conduct

Compliance—the act of adhering to, and demonstrating adherence to, external laws and regulations as well as corporate
policies, procedures, and controls

Basically, GRC rests on the belief that an integrated approach to governance, risk, and compliance can be a valuable tool in avoiding the downsides of risks, including fraud. GRC can be viewed as a system of related functions, with common activities, best approached in a comprehensive, holistic manner.

Since each component of GRC includes numerous sub-processes, it's understandable that fashioning a well-integrated common methodology is considered a daunting task. We don't dispute the notion that developing a robust GRC strategy involves many challenges, but we also believe that GRC is growing in importance and deserves greater attention.

Complicated, but worth the effort

For an expert opinion on the complexities of GRC, we turned to Lee Dittmar, a leading proponent of GRC at Deloitte Consulting LLP.

"Directors, CEOs, CFOs, and leaders everywhere are struggling with ever-increasing challenges as they juggle strategy execution and performance management with myriad risks and complex regulatory requirements in the global marketplace", says Dittmar. "The hard truth is that many executives don't know what they need and want to know — and that's a huge problem."

Many companies may be hard pressed to anticipate and prepare for the multitude of risks generated by the economics of globalization. "Individual and isolated areas of risk exist in abundance, and the resulting complexity is more costly and more risky than necessary or desired", says Dittmar. "The need for and value of implementing an integrated approach to managing the GRC environment is greater than ever."

Despite its complexity, GRC is a challenge worth embracing, and overcoming. We firmly believe that mastering the complexities of GRC can generate business value that is both real and measurable.

Integrated versus nonintegrated GRC

While it might seem obvious that an integrated approach to GRC strategy is preferable to a nonintegrated approach, it's worth a few moments to consider the benefits of integration. The key objectives of integrated GRC include:

- Integrated risk management
- Reduced chance of important risks falling through the cracks by creating a system of checks and balances

- Increased assurance that objectives are met
- Lower costs
- Less duplication of effort and fewer error-prone manual activities
- Reduced need and cost for reconciling information across the company
- Improved business performance
- Improved quality of information upon which decisions are made
- Improved efficiency by optimizing processes to fit collective needs
- Increased profitability providing resources to invest in strategic, long-term objectives.

Survey results show desire for integrated GRC

A 2007 survey of 250 GRC professionals, sponsored by Deloitte LLP, SAP and Cisco, revealed six key areas of agreement on GRC strategy:

1. Integration, maturity and performance go hand in hand.
2. Integration enables efficient and proactive GRC.
3. Integrated GRC creates real business value.
4. Fragmentation is a risky business.
5. Fragmented entities want to change.
6. Everyone expects to spend more money on technologies that will improve their GRC capabilities.

The survey shows that GRC professionals believe strongly that companies with integrated GRC processes perform much better than those whose GRC processes are fragmented. As the survey report states:

> When it comes to risk management, many fragmented entities admit to being behind, and the contrast with integrated entities is dramatic. While fully two-thirds of integrated respondents say they are leaders or better than peers in risk identification and assessment, nearly half of fragmented entities admit to being worse than peers and see that they are lagging behind.

Moreover, the poll indicates that companies with fragmented GRC processes generally skew towards the immature end of the compliance capability scale on every measure.

These are important findings since they seem to suggest a clear message for senior executives when it comes to sorting out GRC priorities. Take advantage of opportunities to integrate GRC processes when they arise.

Key attributes of companies with robust GRC strategies

Our sense is, as we noted in previous chapters, that resilient companies manage the risk of fraud from a strategic point of view. Taking a page from GRC, we would also say that they manage risk in an integrated fashion. Here are some of the key characteristics of resilient corporations with integrated strategies for GRC:

- There is a true balance of power with a proactive, highly independent board operating with objectivity and playing a key role as valued advisors to management.
- Senior management sends a clear and consistent message regarding the company's commitment to responsible and ethical conduct in all dealings and the message is reinforced throughout the company.
- Senior executives and the board embrace risk intelligence as a key principle to help manage performance in all areas.
- Risk is managed using a consistent approach and high-level framework.
- Technology is highly leveraged to automate GRC monitoring, including the use of key performance indicators, and is a key tool used at all levels to manage performance.
- Risk intelligence and GRC are integrated with the company's rewards systems.

As it does with other anti-fraud strategies, internal audit can play an important role as a trusted, objective advisor to management on GRC policies and procedures. Internal audit should also evaluate the design and effectiveness of GRC initiatives.

Even if your company does not embrace GRC, you may well discover that managing ethics, fraud, compliance, and risk management effectively requires careful coordination of people and activities in different departments of your company. Duplicative activities and possibly even turf wars may be an issue, while the risks that fall through the cracks between departments may be less apparent. One way or another, you may well end up pursuing the objectives of GRC, but perhaps in a less ambitious way.

PACI, anti-corruption, and the control environment

As mentioned earlier, a strong control environment also plays a crucial role in deterring corruption. We are all likely to have read about legal remedies against corruption, such as the Foreign Corrupt Practices Act, and its increasing prominence in enforcement circles. Criminalization, however, is not the only anti-corruption strategy for deterring corruption. Management may also be aware of corporate level, self-imposed control programs aimed at combating corruption and its effects.

Companies can enhance their reputation and even gain a competitive advantage by taking a strong stance on anti-corruption. In a September 16, 2008 article in the Nigerian publication *This Day,* Patrick Ugeh reported that the president and CEO of GE International, Ferdinando Nani Beccalli, gave an interview in Abuja in which he stated, "One of the advantages of working with GE is that if you work with GE, you are guaranteed that you are working with a company that is clean, that is not giving bribes and that is always making integrity as the first step in our business. So if the government or anybody cooperates with a company like ours, it is like the seal of guarantee that things are done in a clean way."

With a number of major international companies affected by allegations or investigations of bribery and corruption, winning business under a global media spotlight may increasingly require a strong anti-corruption approach.

The World Economic Forum's Partnering Against Corruption Initiative (PACI) was launched in 2004. It is a private-sector initiative created by the Engineering & Construction, Energy, and Mining & Metals Governors of the World Economic Forum, in cooperation with Transparency International and the Basel Institute on Governance.

Its overarching goal is providing useful guidance on anti-corruption strategies and policies for governments and companies all over the world. As such, it has established a valuable network of corporate relationships with key players and institutions possessing experience and knowledge across a broad range of anti-fraud activities.

PACI has created a set of principles for countering bribery, which includes "a common language on corruption and bribery valid for all industries firmly believing that corruption cannot be countered without leadership and commitment from the top."

Indeed, one of PACI's basic precepts is that corporations should develop a zero-tolerance for bribery. Toward that end, the PACI principles offer a framework for "good business practices and risk management strategies for countering bribery." The principles are designed to help companies:

- Eliminate bribery.
- Demonstrate their commitment to countering bribery.
- Make a positive contribution to improving business standards of integrity, transparency, and accountability whenever they operate.

Because the PACI Principles "are designed to provide companies of all sizes with practical guidance rather than specific prescriptions for developing their own policy statements and programs for combating bribery and other forms of corruption in international business," they are particularly useful and should be considered a valuable set of resources for any company tasked with developing or managing anti-fraud or anti-corruption processes.

It is important for senior executives to understand that PACI, unlike other initiatives, does not focus on the criminal aspects of corruption. It is fundamentally different from a governmental approach to corruption, which centers on enforcement and prosecution. The goal of PACI is helping companies eliminate bribery. It attempts to do so by offering a practical anti-corruption framework that can be implemented from within. In keeping with other aspects of this chapter, one of its key issues is the tone at the top of companies and what that tone says about corruption.

We believe that a resilient corporation would consider integrating the PACI concepts into its existing anti-fraud control environment. As a component of a comprehensive fraud risk management strategy, PACI would likely offer significant benefits to any company that is serious about combating fraud and corruption.

CHAPTER

Preventive Controls: Particular Fraud and Corruption Avoidance Strategies and Tactics

Key points:

➤ In addition to broader, entity-level controls discussed in Chapter 6, effective fraud and corruption risk management also includes the use of controls designed to prevent particular types of fraud and corruption schemes.

➤ The choice of preventive techniques can be driven by the risks identified in the fraud and corruption risk assessment process.

➤ Decisions about whether to implement particular controls may include consideration of the cost-benefit perspective.

➤ Risks change over time. Effective ongoing monitoring allows management to determine whether current controls are still relevant and whether newly identified risks can be managed effectively.

Getting down to brass tacks

Hopefully, what you have read so far has convinced you that a proactive approach to managing fraud and corruption risks offers many advantages. In Chapter 5, we described the fraud and corruption risk assessment process and in Chapter 6 we discussed the importance of the control environment and other corporate wide anti-fraud controls. Now we are going to dive into the details of fraud and corruption controls designed to help prevent particular schemes.

As you probably know, anti-fraud controls are divided into two general categories: preventive and detective. In this chapter, we focus on preventive controls. In Chapter 8, we look at detective controls.

In general, preventive controls are designed to help stop or deter fraud and corruption before it occurs. Since it is reasonable to assume that potential fraudsters will hesitate before committing a wrongful act if they know that specific detective controls are in place; detective controls also can serve as everyday preventive controls. As we will show later in this chapter, detective controls can sometimes serve double-duty as monitoring tools to assess how well the preventive controls are working.

The value of preventive controls can be enormous. In a February 29, 2008 *Chicago Tribune* article by Joshua Boak, a rogue trader in the Memphis office of futures firm MF Global was reported to have made huge unauthorized trades in Chicago wheat futures, leading to a loss of $141.5 million.

According to the article, the company's chief executive said in a conference call with analysts that MF Global had eliminated some trading controls because they slowed the execution process. It was decided after the loss to place controls on all systems, sacrificing some efficiency for security.

Managing the Business Risk of Fraud: A Practical Guide ("the Guide") sums it up neatly in its section on fraud prevention:

> If effective preventive controls are in place, working and well-known to potential fraud perpetrators, they serve as strong deterrents to those who might otherwise be tempted to commit fraud. Fear of getting caught is always a strong deterrent. Effective preventive controls are, therefore, strong deterrence controls.

It is worthwhile to note that the idea of taking a systematic approach to implementing preventive controls is a relatively new development in the evolution of anti-fraud strategy.

Until fairly recently, the accepted approach for dealing with fraud was based to a large degree on finding it after the fact. "We would stumble across fraud while we were looking for something else," is how one expert described the traditional approach.

People generally believed that fraud and corruption were harsh facts of life that you couldn't control, like lightning strikes. As a result, there were few processes for dealing systematically with fraud and corruption, and the processes that did exist were often less than comprehensive.

Contemporary proactive strategies for managing fraud and corruption risks challenge the traditional approach. In essence, the modern strategies focus more effort on preventing and deterring a fraud or corruption scheme from occurring, detecting it as quickly as possible if it occurs, and taking greats steps to mitigate its impact.

There's good reason to be proactive. According to the Association of Certified Fraud Examiners' *2008 Report to the Nation on Occupational Fraud and Abuse,* the median duration of frauds at public companies with whistle-blower hotlines was eight months, or one-third, shorter than at those without hotlines. Even more significantly, the median loss was only $100,000 instead of $784,000, a saving of $684,000 or 87%. That looks like a wise investment, considering a hotline service might cost just a few thousand dollars a year.

Confronting fraud and corruption risks

Fraud controls are devised to confront fraud risks. Like the control environment discussed in the previous chapter, control activities are present across the company, at every level and throughout all functional areas. Their purpose is mitigating fraud and corruption risks that have been identified in the fraud and corruption risk assessment process and ensuring that the company's risk management goals are achieved.

Common wisdom dictates that when fraud and corruption risks are identified, management designs and deploys the controls required to address those identified risks. They can also create additional controls where control activities are nonexistent to address potential risks that become a focus of a fraud and corruption risk assessment. Employees, business process owners, and the internal audit function can all assist in developing these controls.

Companies have often fallen short in confronting fraud and corruption risks due to a misconception that their traditional internal controls will protect them against such risks. Traditional internal controls are not necessarily designed to protect against fraud. According to COSO's definition of internal controls, they are of limited value in fraud prevention due to the key role of collusion, the prominence of management overrides in accounting fraud, and human error.

Another misconception in such companies is the mindset that certain types of fraud, such as those involving collusion and override of controls, can never be prevented or detected. Companies that have been successful in reducing their exposure to fraud have realized that fraud controls can be designed and created, and that traditional controls can be supplemented to help mitigate the risk of fraud.

The Guide illustrates the difference between traditional, general controls and anti-fraud controls: "Where a general, internal control might be executed with limited skepticism (e.g., agreeing an accrual balance to underlying support) an anti-fraud control would include an evaluation of the underlying support for consistency in application from prior periods and for potential inappropriate bias."

Preventive controls can be especially important in difficult economic circumstances or when there is intense pressure to meet expectations. Sometimes the temptation to "fix the numbers" can seem overwhelming. Our colleague, Adam Weisman, puts it this way:

> Every time that you're not meeting expectations, a couple of thoughts probably run through your mind: "What do I do to fix this? How can I meet expectations?" There are ways to meet expectations that are ethically proper and there are ways that are ethically improper. Sometimes if the fix is small, you might be tempted to do something improper. Even when you know it's not ethical, you tell yourself that it's just so unimportant that it really doesn't matter. So you do it. Then the end of next quarter arrives and the expectations have grown. Now the hole that you have to fill is bigger than it was. That's the insidious part about fraud. In order to not get caught for what you did in the previous quarter, you've got to do it again this quarter. And now you have an even bigger hole to fill, so you have to do more things that are probably improper. You find yourself deeper

in the hole and you've got to keep digging in order to not get caught for what you did in the past. It's a vicious cycle.

A vicious cycle indeed. Eventually, a fraudster probably will be caught. By that time, the damage would have been done. If your company had implemented a robust set of preventive controls, one might have thought twice and decided to do the right thing.

Background checks and enhanced due diligence

Preventive controls combating fraud and corruption risks can commence right from the start of employment, at the point of recruiting and hiring potential employees. An anti-fraud preventive measure is to embed fraud controls into the recruiting and hiring process. Companies can do this by assessing candidates from an ethical perspective in the interview screening process. For this to be effective, the company should be prepared to walk away from making an offer to candidates who meet all the requirements of the role but have questionable attitudes toward ethics and integrity.

The University of Notre Dame's Institute for Ethical Business Worldwide has developed ethical guidance for recruiters and job applicants. *Ethical Business Practice: Importance for the Recruiting Process* gives examples of ethics questions recruiters and candidates can ask to help them make an ethically-informed recruiting decision.

In addition, detailed background and reference checks prior to hiring can act as a good fraud preventive control. After the recruiting and hiring process, on-going fraud awareness education, including active education about the red-flags of fraudulent or corrupt activity and measures employees can take to prevent such schemes, can equip employees with knowledge to help prevent and detect fraud and corruption.

Background checks can also be a crucial part of the due diligence process that is a normal part of any proposed acquisition or merger. Our colleague Wendy Schmidt has been retained to conduct extensive background research for global businesses that are interested in acquiring or investing in other businesses, often in distant countries.

"I remember a case involving a large firm that was trying to invest in a smaller company in Southeast Asia. Our research turned up local newspaper stories linking the smaller company to an alleged plot to murder a reporter. Obviously, these were very serious allegations and the firm decided not to invest in the company" says Schmidt.

Automation can be essential

A key consideration for companies in fraud and corruption prevention is the degree of automation of controls. Generally speaking, automated or information technology ("IT") controls are usually better fraud controls than manual controls.

While complete automation of controls is neither practical nor desired, a higher mix of automated versus manual controls usually results in better fraud prevention. Automated controls in the general ledger can identify sensitive or high fraud risk transactions as they happen so that they are flagged for consideration of fraud.

Access controls, meaning restrictions on access to company information based on business needs, are a key example of automated controls. These restrictions are aimed at reducing the risk of individuals accessing certain parts of the company's system to commit fraud. For example, a person who is permitted to make payments for disbursements can be restricted from accessing the general ledger in order to record journal entries. Otherwise, they could initiate a disbursement and then use journal entries to help cover their tracks.

Preventive controls and three broad categories of risk

Preventive fraud controls are generally aligned to confront three broad categories of risk:

1. Fraudulent financial reporting
2. Misappropriation of assets
3. Bribery and corruption

Within each of the three categories there are a number of possible schemes to be considered, including schemes by employees, by customers, by vendors, and by organized criminals. In its *2008 Report to the Nation on Occupational Fraud and Abuse,* the Association of Certified Fraud Examiners sets out its Occupational Fraud and Abuse Classification System. While employee fraud schemes may seem to come in as many different flavors as ice cream, this system demonstrates that in practice, they normally fall into a number of standard varieties. They may be dressed up slightly differently to help deceive the victims, but the core schemes can be remarkably consistent.

This classification system also helps to demonstrate the advantage of organizing your company's potential fraud risks and schemes, taking a complex issue and organizing it into more manageable parts.

"As always, the first step is understanding your business. When you understand your business, you can understand the risks associated with it. Then you can make sure that you have adequate internal controls, along with appropriate policies and procedures, for mitigating those risks," says our colleague Albert Lilienfeld.

Let's now take a deeper dive into some strategies and practices in developing fraud controls for each of these three categories.

Fraudulent financial reporting

One of the most significant concerns in financial reporting relates to the possibility that individuals, often senior executives, may override existing controls in order to report false results. For example, a controller might order an employee of the accounting staff to record in the general ledger a fictitious entry that has no supporting documents and no basis in fact; thereby overriding the normal control of only recording items on the books if there is appropriate supporting documentation. Or a member of the management team intent on committing fraud might violate segregation of duties controls and make journal entries directly into the accounting system.

Examples of fraud controls that may help to mitigate the risk of management override (according to the Public Company Accounting Oversight Board's Auditing Standard No. 5), along with our observations on them, are:

- *Controls over significant, unusual transactions particularly those that result in late or unusual journal entries* These could be special transactions that enable earnings estimates to be met despite adversity in actual business operations. Preventive controls to address such transactions could include required approval of transactions over a certain value by the board and testing of such transactions by internal audit.

- *Controls over journal entries and adjustments made in the period-end financial reporting process* These are manual entries that are made to the books and records after the general journal entries have been processed and closed. An example of such preventive controls would be system restrictions so that such entries require multiple electronic approvals before being processed. They might also be electronically flagged for special attention by the internal audit function.

- *Controls over related party transactions* Controls to prevent fraud in this area could include a mechanism whereby anytime an entry with a related party occurs a flag in the system is set that calls such transactions out and allows for such transactions to be separately viewed, approved and disclosed.

- *Controls related to significant management estimates* These controls reduce the leeway a perpetrator might have to manipulate accounting allowances for bad debts, excess and obsolete inventory, warranty claims, or environmental remediation, for example, thereby achieving the desired bottom line results. Preventive controls here might include well-defined processes for developing and documenting accounting estimates, with testing by the internal audit function of adherence to those processes.

- *Controls that mitigate incentives for, and pressures on, management to falsify or inappropriately manage financial results*—Here the focus is on avoiding compensation mechanisms or performance measures for management that could drive management to commit fraud. Preventive controls here include board review and approval of senior management compensation structures and amounts as well as performance measures, to help avoid undue incentives for fraud.

Misappropriation of assets

Fraud controls in this category vary greatly depending on the industry and the type of assets involved. For many industries, misappropriation of physical assets is a relatively modest risk, occurring quite frequently but in small amounts. Retailers have a more significant issue due to organized retail theft. Technology companies have small high value components that can go astray. And pharmaceutical companies have safety and security issues to consider for certain products in addition to the potential loss of value.

For safeguarding cash, it is particularly important to have good treasury fraud controls. Preventive controls here include strict segregation of duties. Different employees would be responsible for different functions such as approving disbursements and preparing bank reconciliations. More and more companies now have their treasury department separate from their finance department to maintain proper segregation of duties. Strong access controls are also important to help prevent organized criminals on the other side of the world from using online access to empty your company's bank account while you are sound asleep.

A much more challenging area these days is protecting against theft of non-physical or intangible assets such as customer lists, sales records, business plans, and personally identifiable information relating to employees, customers, contractors or others.

A September 17, 2008, article in *American Metal Market* reported that three former employees at auto parts supplier Metaldyne Corp. had pleaded guilty to charges relating to alleged selling of trade secrets to a Chinese competitor. Prosecutors alleged that Metaldyne's former vice president of sales and a metallurgist in the company's Shanghai offices passed information about the company's manufacturing processes and internal costs to the competitor.

As companies go global and stretch their supply chains around the world, the risk of valuable proprietary information being misappropriated increases. Cultural differences and the remoteness of some facilities can render traditional preventive controls less effective.

In this area, strong information security and access controls are key. These might include limiting access to different pools of data, encryption of proprietary customer information, or having a 'sterile' call center environment, meaning one in which no papers or pencils or email access are permitted and information cannot be downloaded to thumb drives or other portable media devices.

Bribery and Corruption

Preventive controls can also be designed to address risks related to corruption. One effective measure is to put in place a program requiring thorough background checks on any joint venture partner, third party agent or vendor prior to doing business with them, including searches on databases of local newspapers and news agencies.

When doing business overseas, it is always good to get feedback from local personnel on the conduct and reputation of potential business partners, agents, or vendors.

A growing practice is also to have a separate ethical code of conduct for vendors, business partners, and agents and having the other party certify adherence to such a code. In addition, contract terms may include provisions on repercussions for bribery and kickbacks and adherence to the Foreign Corrupt Practices Act and other applicable laws and regulations.

To combat the risk of FCPA violations, another control could be to require the review of payments made above a certain threshold to third party agents, government officials, and other politically exposed persons. Such payments can also be subject to an independent review, plus a rule that payments cannot be made outside the country where services are rendered. Such controls may impact the speed and flexibility of doing business, but that may be an acceptable trade-off given the potential downside risks of making inappropriate payments.

Lastly, a good bidding system that requires bids for all procurement activities above a certain dollar threshold can be an effective control. For larger contracts, consider having a cross-functional committee decide which bidders win. This may lessen risks of bribery and kickbacks.

To sum up, each type of control involves costs and trade-offs. Management is responsible for determining which controls are appropriate based on a careful consideration of the potential fraud risks identified in the fraud risk assessment.

Resilient corporations seek to match their fraud controls with their identified risks. They find an efficient balance between preventive and detective controls. Since that balance will shift over time as new tools emerge and risks evolve, be prepared to adjust and refine your preventive controls periodically.

Monitoring and evaluating preventive controls

Monitoring the quality and effectiveness of controls is a critical part of the COSO framework and that applies just as much to fraud controls as to controls designed to prevent and detect errors. While the COSO framework established in 1992 formally introduced the concept of monitoring, in 2009, COSO elaborated on the monitoring component, issuing *Guidance on Monitoring Internal Control Systems.*

This part of COSO had a dual objective: helping companies "improve the effectiveness and efficiency of their internal control systems" and providing "practical guidance that illustrates how monitoring can be incorporated into a company's internal control process."

Stated simply, monitoring helps determine whether your anti-fraud processes are working or need improvement. Monitoring enables you to assess operating effectiveness of controls, identify problems, and report deficiencies.

Monitoring activities consist of independent evaluations and ongoing activities. Independent evaluations are commonly performed by internal audit functions and vary in scope and frequency depending on an assessment of risks and the effectiveness of ongoing monitoring methods. Evaluations can involve implementing detective activities, which are integral as they provide an additional measure of the efficacy of preventative controls.

Detective control processes, which we will focus on in the next chapter, can also help companies identify new fraud risk factors and update their fraud risk assessments. When detective controls identify new schemes that had not been anticipated, new preventative controls can be developed and deployed, creating a dynamic process.

The monitoring process can pay special attention to the risk of override of controls by management. Controls for preventing management override can include active oversight from the audit committee, whistle-blower hotlines and related systems for gathering employee input and reviewing journal entries for evidence of fraud.

Ongoing monitoring takes place within the normal course of business operations. Monitoring activities can include procedures such as the reconciliation of operating and financial reports, recurring reviews and recommendations from internal auditors, and sessions to solicit feedback regarding the effectiveness of controls.

"You don't have to reinvent the wheel," says Mike Novosel, chief audit executive at Chicago-based True Value Company.

You can embed ongoing monitoring within existing processes. For example, we audit lots of corporate processes for Sarbanes-Oxley compliance. I've embedded a piece of monitoring within each of those audits. So when I audit the fixed asset process or the accounts payable process or the accounts receivable process, I do the required 404 key control compliance testing. And then when I'm in front of the people who own that process, I'll ask them about fraud risk. I'll ask if they've had any frauds in the past quarter or the past six months. I'll ask them if there's anything new within their process or in their environment that could make them more vulnerable to fraud. I ask those additional questions, take what I learn and plug it into my ongoing monitoring.

Novosel says he tries not to turn the ongoing monitoring process into another hassle for managers. "I always try to ride the coattails of existing processes that people know and feel comfortable with. So they don't get a memo saying, 'I'm setting up a 30-minute interview to talk with you about fraud risk assessment.' Instead I'll try to get the information I need while I'm talking to them about their 404 compliance work."

We included this anecdote because we believe it illustrates how some management savvy can facilitate a critical process and prevent it from becoming just another tedious chore.

Many monitoring activities can now be automated with the help of newer information technologies. We discuss the role of monitoring along with examples of technologically advanced monitoring tools in depth in Chapter 8.

Continuous controls monitoring

Continuous controls monitoring (CCM) is an example of the newer data-driven technologies used by some companies to enhance their anti-fraud controls systems and processes. Benefits derived from CCM systems include:

- Enhanced capabilities for monitoring internal controls
- Ensuring the appropriate definition and tuning of controls, in part by focusing on control failures and distributing information about them

- Integration of industry best practices with existing company-wide policies
- Greater awareness and increased focus on compliance and standards
- Improved compliance processes
- Better visibility into business and financial data and processes across the company
- Greater efficiency of business and financial processes

CCM systems essentially enable companies to access and monitor crucial data relating to controls more easily and more accurately, providing management with critical information needed for making better business decisions.

For example, if a company is experiencing significantly high volumes of transactional data associated with its travel and entertainment (T&E) systems, CCM technologies and processes could be used to help the company gain greater control and oversight of compliance with its T&E policies. The approach might include:

- Installing and customizing components of a CCM tool, allowing management to receive timely, regular results on the effectiveness of the existing internal controls
- Consolidating the company's disaggregated T&E data into a single, standard form to ensure consistency of data
- Establishing consistent processes, enabling the company to effectively monitor its T&E policies on a continuing basis.

Correcting deficiencies

We believe that employing COSO's monitoring guidance will help companies get their controls working better and lead them to greater levels of resiliency. COSO's *Guidance on Monitoring* sets the expectation for corporations to have monitoring that provides credible information on the effectiveness of the internal control system to key people in the company. Ideally, monitoring can identify and communicate system deficiencies to the people responsible for taking corrective action in a timely manner.

Obviously, the goal here is fixing the control deficiency before an individual or group of individuals exploit it for the purpose of committing fraud or corruption.

The roles of ERM and GRC

We touched briefly on Enterprise Risk Management (ERM) and Governance, Risk and Compliance (GRC) in the previous chapter, but it is worth noting again how both strategies can help companies develop or improve their preventive controls.

It is also important to remember that most successful entrepreneurs consider risk and reward to be proportionally related. The complete absence of risk can remove the potential for profit. It would be unreasonable to expect top managers within companies to be completely deterred by the presence of risk when they perceive opportunities to profit. As some business scenarios become inherently riskier, however, the need for more sophisticated preventive controls is likely to increase.

ERM and GRC are high-level business strategies that place value on superior risk analysis capabilities. From an operational perspective, some of these capabilities can be helpful when companies are trying to identify new risks or gain a better understanding of how particular risks fit into the larger business picture.

As mentioned earlier, using this perspective we refer to companies as "risk intelligent", when they rely on advanced analytic tools and enterprise-level strategies for identifying and assessing risk.

In the context of a discussion about preventive controls, ERM and GRC can help companies find emerging risks and develop effective controls to reduce the potential for harm.

In general, resilient corporations are highly effective and efficient in managing risks to both existing assets and to future growth. In our belief, they will, in the long run, outperform companies that manage the risks of fraud and corruption less effectively or efficiently.

CHAPTER

8

Detective Controls and Transaction Monitoring

Key points:

➤ The main lesson is that monitoring for fraud and corruption is everyone's business.

➤ Monitoring and detection come in a variety of forms, from checks performed by internal audit, to tipster hotlines, to the periodic review of particular transactions, to continuous monitoring of transactions.

➤ The sheer volume of data that companies must process, screen, sort, and protect demands ever-more-powerful tools to address fraud and corruption in real time.

➤ Monitoring and detection tools are becoming increasingly prominent components of strong fraud and corruption risk management strategies.

➤ Advanced technologies are playing larger roles in fraud and corruption monitoring and detection.

➤ More companies are using continuous monitoring techniques to detect and respond to fraud on a near real-time basis.

The importance of monitoring and detection

Despite the measures we discussed in the previous two chapters, frauds can and do still occur. In this chapter, we discuss the importance of using detection techniques to attempt to identify the frauds and instances of corruption that are committed despite controls. This discussion is necessarily oriented to particular schemes and particular instances. Because previous chapters were about controls, we spoke of monitoring, or observing, and testing controls to determine whether they are working as intended or could be improved. When we speak of monitoring here we do so in a different way than in the previous chapters. Here we mean monitoring particular transactions to determine whether they are indicative of fraud or corruption schemes.

Most of the frauds we know about have been discovered either by tips or by people stumbling over them. In what is probably the most comprehensive study of how frauds come to be known, the Association of Certified Fraud Examiners' *2008 Report to the Nation on Occupational Fraud & Abuse,* shows that 46 percent of the frauds studied were learned about through tips, 23 percent through internal controls, 20 percent were discovered accidentally, and just under 20 percent were detected by internal audits (the total exceeds 100 percent because multiple detection methods could be reported for a single fraud).

It is our experience that knowledge of the fraud often begins with an unusual event or unexplained action. In the case of the tip, a fellow employee might see a colleague do something unusual with a procurement situation, perhaps avoiding a control, and then report that. In the instance of an accidental discovery, a clerk might be trying to reconcile accounts and can't find a way to do that within usual business boundaries. Digging deeper, the clerk might find an entry to the books that does not follow procedure and is suspicious.

One premise of this book is that with the right fraud and corruption risk management strategy in place, more frauds and instances of corruption can be prevented or identified through controls. However, controls will get us only so far. We also recognize that what we do not stop or find through the normal course of business, still might be a problem. For this reason, companies can encourage a skeptical attitude on the part of employees in order to promote tips, adequately promote and fund their internal audit function, and explore the use of active detective controls, such as transaction monitoring, where possible.

The ACFE's report indicates that the median duration of an occupational fraud is two years. The Deloitte Forensic Center's 2008 study of financial statement frauds found that, on average, the time between when frauds began and when the SEC published its most recent enforcement release was 6.3 years. Bigger frauds tead to be more time-consuming and more costly to resolve. Anything a company can do to shorten the period of loss and the time spent resolving such issues can translate directly into money saved and profit.

Monitoring and detection tactics

In this chapter, we profile several key monitoring and detection tactics. This discussion is not meant to be either exhaustive or a roadmap. Rather, we are providing an overview and an introduction to a number of what we perceive to be the more interesting tactics.

We begin with a number of considerations regarding whistle-blower hotlines. We have already noted the role of tips in uncovering frauds, the Sarbanes-Oxley requirement for companies to employ hotlines, and the recent guidance on hotline effectiveness. In this chapter we focus on the major issues regarding hotlines.

Next, we describe the role internal audit can play in conducting fraud risk based audits and the benefits internal auditors can provide in terms of fraud risk management.

We then turn to monitoring tactics. First, we discuss manual monitoring, then we turn to the use of technology in managing fraud–risks by considering electronic transaction review and monitoring, as well as continuous fraud monitoring. The latter is of particular interest, because it has the promise of stopping some fraud and corruption schemes before they have effect.

Whistle-blower hotlines

It is easy to put a whistle-blower hotline in place, but more difficult to establish one that works and has the confidence of executives and employees.

In a 2007 study by the Deloitte Forensic Center, only 32 percent of the executives surveyed believed their whistle-blower hotlines were very effective. Since hotlines are a critical part of compliance, ethics and fraud risk management programs, executives' lack of confidence in them suggests improvements may be widely needed.

Audit committees, boards of directors, and senior executives may wish to look into the performance of their company's hotline. Asking the following questions may help identify performance improvement opportunities.

How does our hotline's performance compare to industry-specific benchmarking data?

Ideally, you would benchmark your hotline annually using industry-specific statistics for performance measures such as call volume, call mix, anonymity usage, and prior notification of management. Usage varies considerably by industry, which makes using industry-specific benchmarking data important.

According to the *2007 Corporate Governance and Compliance Hotline Benchmarking Report,* published by Security Executive Council, an average hotline might generate around eight incident reports per 1,000 employees on an annual basis (e.g., if there are 20,000 employees, you might expect around 160 incident reports per year). There may be lower call volumes for companies with high volumes of unionized or international workers due to cultural differences or preferences for alternative reporting mechanisms. However, low usage is not necessarily better. It may signal that a company is failing to promote an ethical culture and that personnel do not feel comfortable reporting issues without fear of retribution, or the company is failing in its communication efforts.

Have we surveyed employees' willingness to use the hotline?

Insights into the effectiveness of the whistle-blower reporting mechanism can be gained by surveying employees to measure their willingness to use the hotline and their degree of trust in management to resolve issues appropriately and not to take retribution against those who report wrongdoing. Evaluating the survey results by operating unit or by geographic area can identify areas where the hotline may be less effective or not effective at all, enabling you to implement appropriate remediation.

How do we communicate and promote use of the hotline?

It is not enough to set up an 800 number or website and expect employees to start asking their questions or making reports. To be effective, employees need to know the hotline is available and why and when they should use it. Successful and widelyused hotlines are generally promoted through a regular communication and education program, which may include such mechanisms as wallet cards, newsletters, posters, codes of ethics, payroll inserts, screensavers, giveaways such as pens, and calculators, interest messaging, new-hire training, and ethics training. Ultimately, the goal would be for all personnel to know there is a hotline and how they can access it. The company can determine how to communicate that message within its corporate culture in order for the hotline to be effective.

Do we use a reputable third-party hotline provider?

A company could set up a hotline system of its own in-house or it can obtain that service from a reputable third party. Using a third party for a hotline involves having an independent organization receive inquiries or reports of incidents (through phone and Web-based reporting). Typically, a company's ethics and compliance officer is responsible for overseeing the investigation and resolution of all issues raised. The advantages of using a third-party professional to provide the hotline may include extended hours of availability, increased perception of confidentiality, and reduced cost. While absolute confidentiality cannot be guaranteed even with an outsourced hotline, the third-party alternative has the advantage of being an objective contractor who can help alleviate fear of retribution and help reduce concerns about confidentiality and anonymity.

A key advantage of using a reputable third-party hotline provider is that there may be greater confidence by the board and audit committee that reports of potential wrongdoing involving senior management or financial reporting will be communicated by the third-party provider directly to the audit committee or board of directors, in accordance with established protocols, without the opportunity for inappropriate intervention by senior management. While some companies' ethics officers or ombudsmen may have reporting lines to the board or audit committee to provide a comparable function, concerns may arise about hotlines overseen by senior executives who report up to the CEO.

Does our hotline provider offer industry-leading capabilities?

There are many important issues in selecting a hotline provider. They include finding vendors for whom hotlines are a core business, whether the service is 24/7 and is staffed with live interviewers, whether it includes foreign language support and international calling, the nature of interviewer training and the documentation of procedures, accuracy and speed of dissemination of incident reports, whether reports are available online, case management capabilities, system security considerations, and, of course, short-term and long-term cost.

Risk-based internal audits as a fraud detection tactic

Internal audits are a key way in which companies seek to detect fraud and corruption, even though an increasing amount of fraud and corruption detection work is also being done by operating departments, as line managers take on more responsibility for managing fraud risks in their business unit.

Internal auditors play a critical role in performing proactive fraud and corruption detection work at the direction of the audit committee or the board of directors. This work is likely to be targeted at key risks such as avoiding the risk of management override of internal controls. Since management should not be given the task of checking itself, due to conflicts of interest, this is appropriately a role for the internal audit function.

Although the audit committee and the board may not expect management overrides of internal controls to occur, they may find significant value in having the internal audit function conduct testing to detect such overrides. Such testing can have a deterrent effect on management as well as increasing the opportunity to detect overrides and take corrective action where necessary.

Internal auditors can also play a valuable role in identifying potential flaws in business processes and in internal controls over those processes. As we discussed toward the end of Chapter 5, computer-assisted auditing techniques and continuous monitoring can be very effective in scanning large volumes of transactions and identifying a small subset that exhibit anomalies. These can then be evaluated by internal auditors who can consider whether the anomalies arise from normal operations and variations, or are due to errors, or perhaps are indicative of fraud.

A key consideration in this type of work is balancing cost and benefit. The goal here is not to chase down every $25 fraud. It is to continuously improve business processes and controls so as to achieve the control objectives in a cost-effective manner. Identifying vulnerabilities in business processes and weaknesses in controls is valuable if it enables them to be addressed before they are exploited to commit either large frauds or numerous small ones that will collectively be costly.

The role of internal auditors in addressing fraud risks has been enhanced by changes to the Institute of Internal Auditors' International Standards for the Professional Practice of Internal Auditing (the "Standards"), which took effect January 1, 2009. A new Standard, 2120.A2, states:

> The internal audit activity must evaluate the potential for the occurrence of fraud and how the organization manages fraud risk.

This standard requires internal auditors to evaluate fraud risks at their company. A revision to Standard 2210.A2 requires that knowledge be put to work when designing the objectives of every internal audit performed. The revised Standard states:

> The internal audit activity must consider the probability of significant errors, fraud, noncompliance, and other exposures when developing the engagement objectives.

With this Standard, internal auditors are explicitly required to consider the probability of fraud in a particular area when they develop their plans for an internal audit of that area. This change may lead to greater integration of fraud detection into the everyday routine of internal auditors.

Manual monitoring

While the use of technology-based tools for detecting fraud and corruption is expanding, there remains an important role for manual monitoring.

Large volumes of similar transactions are well suited to automated monitoring, but smaller volumes of transactions of many different kinds, especially high-value or high-risk items, may currently be more easily addressed through manual monitoring.

Financial statement fraud, for example, can be committed in many different ways and many different types of transactions are processed through a company's accounting system. While software will likely become increasingly available to screen for potential signs of fraud in certain types of transactions, such as revenue recognition items or journal entries, manual monitoring still has a valuable role to play in detecting fraud and errors in operating reports and financial statements.

In larger organizations with many operating units, regional or divisional financial managers who analyze financial reports from individual units play an important role in detecting fraudulent financial reporting being committed by managers in charge of particular entities. Their experience at analyzing reports, frequently from the same entities, and their evaluation of the responses given by local management to questions raised, can equip them to identify anomalies that might otherwise go undetected.

The effectiveness of such manual monitoring can be impacted by office politics. Strong support from senior management may be vital to overcome obstructionist or unresponsive tactics by business unit managers trying to avoid well-aimed questions and conceal their actions.

Technology-based detection tactics

Thanks to the emergence of various new technologies, many essential monitoring activities can be strengthened and automated at reasonable cost. Solutions for continuous monitoring, continuous auditing, employee testing-and data mining/data analytics are widely available from numerous vendors.

The extremely rapid adoption of digital information systems by companies of all sizes has fueled the explosive growth of technology-driven processes such as data mining and data analytics. This growth has been accelerated by continuously declining prices of computer hardware (a working example of Moore's Law, which says that computer capacities at minimum cost increase exponentially) and the swift development of new software applications to meet increasing market demand.

Data mining uses powerful software to sift through terabytes of data and billions of transactions stored in data warehouses and other data storage centers. Data analytics relies on highly sophisticated programs that sort through mountains of information in search of unseen patterns that might suggest wrongdoing or other issues worth investigating. Analytics can also help companies build test models and strengthen systems for monitoring and detecting anomalous or suspicious activities.

Bill Coleman, audit compliance manager at Pfizer Inc., illustrates the extent of testing that can be accomplished using technology but that would be prohibitively time-consuming and costly to perform manually; "We took our database of 300,000 vendors and matched them against our 200,000 colleagues to look for conflicts of interest," he said. "For example, vendors that have the same addresses or phone numbers as employees. You can look for vendors with no phone numbers. Do they have a tax ID number, and if they don't have one, why not? Tax ID numbers that match employees' social security numbers; those are the types of cross referencing that are a great thing to do," he added.

However, for data mining to be effective in the struggle against fraud, an antecedent consideration must be addressed. Steps must be taken to ensure the adequacy of data, which translates into the need to maintain data integrity, security, and accuracy.

Indeed, data integrity has become a priority for companies large and small. Data that is entered, converted, stored, or reported must meet the highest standards of quality and integrity. But many companies do not possess the capabilities required to ensure the reliability of their data, especially when dealing with intricate business processes, applications, and complex data requirements.

This inability to assess the quality of data can be disastrous to an enterprise-wide anti-fraud strategy that relies on sophisticated information technologies and advanced software solutions such as data mining, data analytics, and continuous controls monitoring.

We believe that corporations using sophisticated data interrogation and analysis, statistical sampling, and regression techniques to assess the accuracy and integrity of system data quickly and cost effectively are more likely to be resilient when faced with the threat of fraud and corruption. They develop in-house capabilities or reach out to external resources to acquire the combination of analytical skills and IT knowledge necessary to make certain that data is accurate, timely, secure, and accessible to authorized users when they need it.

Examples of fraud detection using data interrogation techniques

Many companies today extract data from their systems and perform tests to determine if there is evidence of foul play. In this section, we briefly describe four examples of testing in order to provide an overview of what is an increasingly large and complex group of technology-based anti-fraud and corruption detection techniques that companies may use. These techniques cover many types of schemes. They range from procurement fraud, accounting fraud, anti-money laundering, and corruption, to such things as credit card fraud and checking for fraudulent medical claims.

The monitoring we describe can be carried out by business units, compliance groups, or internal audit, each working in conjunction with the IT group.

Monitoring to detect procurement fraud

Procurement fraud poses a risk to many companies. It consists of schemes perpetrated by employees that have the effect of defrauding the company. The schemes, which are sometimes carried out alone and other times in collusion with third parties, often involve employees entering fake vendors in the accounts payable system, then paying the vendor's false bills to accounts controlled by the employee or colluding entity.

The garden variety of procurement schemes can be detected by such techniques as comparing vendor addresses to employee addresses, or vendor bank accounts to employee bank accounts. These are relatively simple searches and may be periodically undertaken by companies. Other red flag items can also be determined electronically, by, for example, comparing data in the vendor file with third-party data. Third-party data can provide reverse directory information or can verify tax identification numbers.

A more difficult to detect version of the scheme occurs when employees change the vendor's address to an address they control and then submit false invoices. This version of the scheme can be detected by culling the group of transactions that involve both payments and antecedent address changes.

Paul Lucas, Chief of Investigations Branch for the United Nations Population Fund, is an enthusiastic user of automated transaction monitoring. "In the early stages we installed some monitoring software on the ERP system," he states. "That's picked up for us some of the biggest anomalies, usually around the payment cycle."

More difficult still are frauds based on collusion. These often involve the violation of procurement rules by favoring vendors (providing them with competitor's prices, for example) and kickbacks to the employee from the favored vendor. Such situations are usually not apparent in the company's records. Detecting them often begins with complaints from losing vendors and/or tips. The data work lies in investigating the complaint and/or the tip. For example, using data interrogation techniques to review communications, such as emails, can supplement other techniques such as reviewing the personal finances of the suspected employees, if the company requires mandatory financial disclosures and audit rights as a condition for employment, for unexplained income.

Monitoring to detect financial statement fraud

Financial statement frauds are one of the dangers a company may face. The Deloitte Forensic Center's 2008 study of financial statement frauds alleged in SEC Accounting and Auditing Enforcement Releases showed that a large proportion involve manipulating revenue recognition. This can be carried out by making false entries in consolidated results toward the end of reporting periods. Other things we know about such entries from experience is that they are often made after hours or on weekends and can be made by higher level personnel. Also, there is sometimes a reversing entry after reports are issued.

Detecting such entries, if they occur, can begin with identifying rules that specify the data conditions to search for and then extracting the accounting data that will be searched. In the simple example, the company would search for a number of data conditions: journal entries made around reporting periods, after hours, or on weekends, journal entries made by high level employees, and journal entries that are reversed in the following reporting periods.

There is an investigative function that must be a part of electronic detection techniques like this one. The transactions that qualify would normally need to be further reviewed before there is a conclusion that they are, in fact, indicative of fraud.

Monitoring to detect money laundering

Violations of anti-money laundering laws take many forms and, even more so than the other types of transaction monitoring we discuss here, have a needle-in-the-haystack aspect. For most companies facing compliance with anti-money laundering laws, such as banks, and especially clearing banks, millions and billions of transactions may have to be reviewed. It seems clear that using computer technology is usually the only way to accomplish the monitoring that must be done.

As is widely known, banks in the U.S. must report on certain transactions greater than $10,000. Those that are intent on avoiding the attention reporting could entail, sometimes use a technique called "structuring," in which a number of smaller transactions are made which when combined equal a sum equal to or greater than $10,000.

Banks and other financial institutions have developed computer search techniques to monitor for the possibility of structuring (as is also the case with anti-corruption monitoring, as noted below). Transactions between parties within time parameters are analytically combined by computer systems to look for instances in which structuring may have occurred.

The computer system reports out the flagged transactions, which must then be reviewed by bank personnel to determine whether a suspicious activity report must be filed with the appropriate governmental agency.

Monitoring to detect FCPA and other corruption violations

Violations of the U.S. Foreign Corrupt Practices Act and other types of corruption usually take the form of bribes paid to government officials by company officials, employees, or agents. The bribes can be paid in many ways, and, these days, are usually hidden as legitimate transactions. For example, they might be called "tuition payments", or they might be structured into a number of smaller expense report transactions that collectively equal the sum of the bribe. Sometimes they appear as agreements for seemingly legitimate services. In the case of the Oil-for-Food Programme, many of the companies that paid bribes to Saddam Hussein's government did so after agreeing, in side contracts, to pay "after-service sales fees," which turned out to be bogus and simply bribes.

Based on data developed over the course of many corruption investigations in our experience, the characteristics of bribes and bribe payments are better understood than they were previously. For example, most bribe payments are in even amounts, say $5 million, and are paid outside the normal accounts payable functions through journal entries in ledgers. Typically, they are paid to nonestablished vendors. To monitor for bribe payments, a company can query its payments for those that are in even numbers, or that have been structured to produce even numbers. It can also review the text in journal entries, using text processing and searching software, to look for any number of terms designed to mislead, like tuition. Lastly, it can examine the list of parties to whom it has made payments and determine whether likely bribe recipients are included (by, for example, comparing the list to databases of politically exposed persons maintained by third parties).

Once candidate transactions have been identified they must be explored and qualified by examining the underlying accounting, contractual, and documentary information, in keeping with all other forms of electronic detection. Increasingly, these checks are initially conducted by the business units involved, then they are elevated to compliance or investigation units if the facts warrant.

Continuous fraud monitoring

Fraud detection tools have evolved significantly over the past 15 years. Prior to the widespread adoption of digital information systems, almost all fraud detection involved the manual review of paper documents and spreadsheet analysis.

As fraud detection moved into the digital age, desktop databases enabled transaction sampling and database analysis into areas like the ones described above. More recently, server-based databases enabled full transaction review and more robust analysis of larger databases.

Within the past few years, web-based front-end systems and other newer technologies have enabled what we know today as *continuous fraud monitoring*, or CFM. With CFM, management can put in place exacting transaction-by-transaction reviews according to rules-based systems. They can also perform near-real-time examinations of the transactions flagged to identify potential problems quickly and generate the appropriate response.

CFM differs from continuous controls monitoring (CCM) technologies discussed in the previous chapter in that it focuses on identifying transactions that qualify as violations of rules or that qualify as exceptions or outliers based on statistical or mathematical tests. The goal of CFM is to identify the transactions used to carry out fraud schemes or to engage in corrupt behavior. For example, an accounting system might have a module that tests all journal entries for after hour or weekend timestamps and reports the transactions that qualify for review. This test is based on the fact noted above: Entries in accounting frauds are often made outside normal business routines and after hours. CCM, on the other hand, as we have seen, is focused on the performance of controls, by developing statistics about rule violations.

CFM also differs from older, discrete fraud detection processes in several important ways. Discrete fraud detection is generally based on periodic reviews recurring every year, month, or week, depending on the application. Essentially, it consists of taking a "snapshot" of selected transactions at a moment in time and then reviewing the data for signs of fraud schemes. While it can be performed manually or automatically, it usually requires a new data feed or data extraction each time it is performed. Moreover, not all transactions are subject to review, either due to timing or sampling constraints.

On the other hand, CFM relies on a near-real-time surveillance system to identify anomalies and handle them instantaneously, either by not allowing fraudulent transactions to be executed or by flagging them and tagging them with a risk score so they can be reviewed by appropriate personnel as soon as they are detected.

CFM systems can be rules-based (which means they are programmed to reflect common-sense rules of accounting), they can be based on artificial intelligence (AI) technologies, or they can be a hybrid combining features of both rules-based and AI approaches.

Because CFM is an information technology-driven business process, it is capable of performing real-time monitoring of accounting systems and transactions to detect and address fraudulent activity. Ideally, CFM can be used to identify particular fraud schemes before they take effect.

A CFM system is intended to catch the anomalies in accounting systems, as defined by rules or algorithms, flag them, and route them to the appropriate person with suggestions for how to address the anomaly.

Potential advantages of continuous fraud monitoring processes:

- Identify fraudulent activities that traditional monitoring processes are less likely to find, due to their episodic nature or sampling techniques.
- Discover transactional information that reflects an attempt to cover tracks, such as certain forms of reversing entries.
- Reveal intentional splits of transactions across multiple time periods.
- Shortens time between the commission of a fraud and review that might uncover it.
- Reduces time that fraudsters have to cover up their improper activities.
- Reduce the chances of transactions being overlooked or omitted during traditional monitoring processes.
- Reduce impact of fraud by bringing it to light sooner and avoiding secondary effects.
- Enable tighter integration with business operations.
- Reduce costs associated with data extraction, delivery, and loading.

Is CFM for everyone?

Increased computing speeds, greater storage capacity, and other improvements in enterprise-level information technologies suggest that CFM is likely to play a greater role in the anti-fraud strategies of large companies, and companies operating in especially complex markets.

That being said, it is also important to understand that not every company needs a comprehensive CFM system. Large, high-volume businesses such as banks and other financial institutions, healthcare companies, and certain types of multinational corporations are likely candidates for CFM implementations.

How can you tell whether your company can reasonably expect to benefit from an investment in CFM technology? Here are three questions you can ask yourself:

1. Does the company have enough transaction flow to justify the effort?
2. Does the company have the resources necessary to commit the time, energy and money required for implementing a CFM system?
3. Does the company have an internal audit function that is independent and experienced enough to interpret and respond effectively to anomalies as they are identified by a CFM system?

The importance of lookbacks as a control check

There is another important point to make about CFM solutions, and in fact about any control regimen that relies on transaction monitoring. Like any control mechanism, CFM and other computerized monitoring systems must be reviewed for their effectiveness. Are they finding the transactions they are intended to identify? Are they reporting more transactions than they are intended to identify?

To answer these and other questions, companies often rely on what has come to be called *lookbacks*. In a lookback, the company probes historical data, after first building a data warehouse, using a variety of sophisticated search techniques, to determine whether suspicious transactions have gone unreported. This technique is also used to address the question of whether false positive rates are appropriate or excessive.

In some industries, financial services for example, regulators require lookbacks if they have a question about the number of suspicious activity reports a company has filed.

Questions to ask about monitoring and detection

1. Does the audit committee have oversight of monitoring activities?
2. Does management assess the design and operating effectiveness of monitoring activities?
3. Does management adequately document its assessments and conclusions regarding the design and operating effectiveness of the monitoring activities?
4. Has adequate attention been paid to employing the detection strategies available?
5. Is the internal audit group adequate for the size, complexity, and risk profile of the company?
6. Is there an adequate, properly functioning tipster hotline in place?
7. Is management reviewing the results of incidence reports from the hotline or from other detection tests?
8. Are controls being monitored for their effectiveness in managing fraud and corruption risks?
9. Is there a handoff to an investigation group or function to ensure that incidents flagged are properly addressed?
10. Are findings and weaknesses identified during monitoring activities incorporated back into the fraud and corruption risk assessment, the design of the control environment, and anti-fraud control activities?

CHAPTER 9

Preparing for Fraud and Corruption Investigations and Remediation

Key points:

➢ A crucial objective of a fraud and corruption risk management strategy is mitigating the impact of frauds and instances of corruption once they occur.

➢ Fraud investigation can help to restore confidence and reputation, while providing valuable information to improve business processes and strengthen controls.

➢ Anticipate that investigations of significant frauds or corruption will be subject to intense scrutiny.

➢ Identifying in advance the resources to be used to investigate significant frauds can speed the response in a crisis.

➢ Establishing investigation protocols in advance can help to avoid missteps that can cause reputational harm.

➢ Newer technologies exist, such as remote data collection, to help with some of the key steps in investigations.

Be prepared

By now, we hope that you have accepted our basic premise that since fraud cannot be completely eradicated, wisdom suggests that preparedness is the best strategy to deal with the frauds that may occur. Resilient corporations accept the reality that fraud will occur, and they take steps to make certain they are ready to respond effectively when it does.

"It is fair to say that fraud investigations have become much larger and much more complex than they were in the past," notes our colleague, Bill Pollard. "The fraud schemes themselves have not changed that much, but I think they have become more sophisticated and more pervasive. So, there is a greater burden to carry when you are doing an investigation."

In many instances, the way a company investigates an incident of fraud can be just as critical—and sometimes even more critical—than the fact that the fraud took place.

"I know of a company where allegations were not all that significant," recalls Pollard, "but the company had no records-retention policy. They kept everything. And as a result, they were forced to spend millions of dollars combing through old records. If they had anticipated this risk, they could have avoided a substantial cost by putting a retention policy in place."

The lesson, says Pollard, is that "nobody is immune. You have to understand that you could be susceptible to an investigation at any time. So you have to think strategically and follow a prudent document retention policy."

We will now look at some practical strategies for avoiding some of the common pitfalls that can occur when preparing for and conducting corporate investigations. We will also discuss how some companies get more value out of their investigations and use them more effectively to help prevent future issues.

In our experience, we have observed that resilient corporations adopt careful, disciplined approaches to all steps of an investigation. They do not rush to conclusions in an effort to save time or money as such behavior can lead to incomplete or erroneous conclusions, as well as raise doubts about whether the allegations have been fully explored. They also place strong emphasis on identifying the vulnerabilities in business processes and internal controls that permitted the wrongdoing and they work to remediate them across their entire company.

Managing the Business Risk of Fraud: A Practical Guide (the "Guide") provides a useful overview of recommended practices for conducting investigations and taking corrective actions.

The Guide suggests that the board of directors take responsibility for seeing that the company develops "a system for prompt, competent, and confidential review, investigation, and resolution of allegations involving potential fraud or misconduct."

The Guide also shares leading practices for receiving, responding to, and evaluating allegations of fraud. Furthermore, it recommends specific tasks for conducting an investigation, including interviewing, evidence collection, computer forensic examinations, and evidence analysis.

In our experience, some of the opportunities for companies to enhance their processes in this area include:

- Identifying fraud and corruption investigation resources, especially global response teams, in advance of a crisis
- Establishing and documenting fraud and corruption investigation protocols
- Implementing a case management system to track and log allegations of fraud and corruption and their resolution
- Implementing automated tools for collecting electronic information in regulatory investigations and litigations
- Drawing on the results of investigations into instances of fraud and corruption allegations at one's own company or more generally in an industry to implement process and control improvements enterprise-wide to gain efficiencies and prevent recurrences

An ounce of planning . . .

Since the impact of fraud and corruption cases can be very significant and time may be of the essence in resolving them, it is prudent to make sure that your response plans are in place beforehand. When the board of directors, audit committee, regulators, or the news media suddenly want to know what management is doing to resolve new allegations of wrongdoing, you will be glad you have a response plan already prepared and in motion.

In addition to planning an initial response to a fraud allegation, resilient corporations generally also set in place processes for communicating information about the fraud, and about the corporation's response, to the various involved parties. This process of communicating is more complicated than you might expect, due in part to the tension between the need to calm constituents and the lawyers' likely preference to reveal relatively little. It would be unwise to leave the development of the communication process until the last moment.

The planning process also includes steps to take, depending on the conditions related to the alleged incident's facts, scope, nature, and timing.

Some companies train or hire crisis management teams before a crisis occurs; others wait until the crisis is upon them. We think it is prudent to prepare and to plan internally for the worst, especially if your company is large with much shareholder value at stake.

As part of your response plan, you should consider establishing predetermined roles and responsibilities for management, legal counsel, the audit committee, the board and other key functions within the corporation. Cases of alleged fraud or corruption involving senior management or financial reporting will likely have to be handled by the audit committee or a special committee of the board. In addition, there would typically be a policy to notify the audit committee and the external auditors immediately for any allegations relating to financial statements or internal controls.

What to do when regulators come knocking . . .

Sometimes your company will receive allegations and be in charge of initiating an internal investigation. At other times, the first you learn of an issue may be when the government comes knocking at your door. How a company responds to an external investigation can be as important as the underlying issue being investigated.

"Mishandling a government investigation can cause more problems than the original issue," says Barry Goldsmith, partner and co-chair of Gibson, Dunn & Crutcher LLP's Securities Enforcement Practice Group, and a member of that firm's Securities Litigation Practice Group and White Collar Defense and Investigations Practice Group.

"It is critical to have a logical and effective response plan—if not in place already, at least prepared quickly after notice is received," says Goldsmith, a former executive vice president for enforcement at the National Association of Securities Dealers and the chief litigation counsel for the SEC.

Ideally, the response plan would include an analysis of the documents requested by the government. Sometimes you can gain helpful insight by re-examining what has been examined by government investigators. You can also find out how the government has proceeded in similar cases. Knowing how the government has acted in the past might provide valuable clues about how it might act in your case.

It is also good practice to develop your own set of suggested solutions to remediate the problems or issues under investigation. Some companies have preemptively drawn up lists of limitations and remedial actions they are willing to consider. This approach may appeal to the general desire of most regulators to seek solutions.

At all points in the fact-gathering process, the guiding principles would generally be responsiveness and helpfulness.

Evaluating the allegation

Not every allegation requires a full-blown investigation. A preliminary analysis may indicate that the situation is a misunderstanding, that the facts do not support the allegation, or that that there is insufficient information to enable an effective investigation to be conducted.

But one should not write-off allegations prematurely. Establishing a formal process for evaluating allegations of wrongdoing, whether received through the company's whistle-blower hotline or otherwise, is a prudent practice. A small group of individuals can be assigned to that role to help achieve consistency and provide coverage at all times. The company's general counsel or designee might lead that process with participation from the director of internal audit or the director of fraud/security, depending on which group typically handles day-to-day investigations in the company.

A senior representative of the human resources (HR) function might also participate since many allegations involve HR issues, and they can provide valuable insights on other cases, too.

Our colleague, Gerry Fujimoto, is an experienced forensic investigator and he offered some suggestions to help guide the decision-making processes around fraud investigations. "The company's internal counsel and internal auditors are often the principal players in the early phase of an investigation," says Fujimoto. "Their goal should be to gather all necessary information about the allegation so they can make an informed decision on how the investigation should move forward."

Fujimoto recommends that key players evaluate the quality and quantity of the information that is known, including who raised the concern—for example, anonymous, or someone in a position to be knowledgeable about the issue—as well as how much information is presently known, and whether it is a specific or general allegation.

Be careful not to make potentially false assumptions about the scope and scale of the problem. "In our experience," Fujimoto says, "if there is any merit to the matter at all, it tends to grow in size, number of issues and value."

It is important to respond quickly and without delay. Fujimoto advises not to take a wait-and-see approach. "This usually does not sit well with a number of parties who are interested in the investigation, including your external auditors, regulatory agencies such as the SEC, and the person who initially raised the allegations."

Assembling the right investigation team

When potential accounting or financial reporting irregularities are suspected, it is recommended that the audit committee or a special committee of the board oversee the investigation, to help avoid potential conflicts of interest with members of management. The investigation would typically be led by independent counsel, who can ensure that the engagement has the strongest legal protections and that relevant legal and regulatory implications are considered. "If the concern raised relates to an accounting or financial reporting matter, the people performing the initial steps should be disinterested parties," says Fujimoto.

Since the goal is to conduct an investigation that will have credibility and stand up to external scrutiny, consider the skills and experiences of the individuals on your team. Be prepared, if necessary, to reach out to external resources with special skills for gathering or evaluating certain types of information.

"At the conclusion of the investigation," says Fujimoto, "your company will want to be able to thoroughly describe to the SEC, other regulators, and other interested parties exactly what happened. Based on findings, you should also be able to identify remedial actions to be taken. This can help you get the right internal controls in place and also help restore public confidence."

The organization and structure of an internal investigation response team can be critical, says our colleague Kerry Francis, chairman of the board of Deloitte Financial Advisory Services LLP.

For example, if the allegation is related to financial reporting (but does not include allegations against management), you would expect to see someone from internal audit with a finance/accounting background participating in the investigation. Who will be ultimately responsible for the investigation oversight is another key concern. Is it the Audit Committee, the Board of Directors, or those in management who are not implicated in the allegation?

A key tactical question to consider is whether the individual members of the internal investigation team have been trained to conduct investigations, says Francis. "Do they understand chain of custody issues? Have they been trained to use the appropriate technologies? Do they know how to conduct a proper interview? Are they acquiring data properly? Are they analyzing data and facts appropriately? These are the questions that a company can answer to prepare itself in advance for conducting internal investigations."

When to call for help

We have observed that an essential aspect of corporate resiliency is to know when to escalate responses to crises. Resilient corporations develop decision-making procedures that enable them to determine when it may be necessary to call in external resources such as forensic accountants and when it may be adequate to rely on internal resources. Here is a brief list of criteria a company may consider during the decision-making process:

- Could the company's financial statements be affected by the fraud allegations?
- Are company officers or other senior executives potentially involved?
- Will the allegations hurt the company's brand or diminish its reputation?
- What is the probability of the fraud allegations being disclosed to the public?

Not every situation rises to the level of concern that requires outside assistance. For example, everyday embezzlement cases can often be handled by suitably trained internal resources such as fraud and security personnel or internal auditors, working under the direction of in-house counsel.

As the potential impact (not just the amount) of the alleged fraud or corruption grows, or as more senior people are potentially touched by the allegations, so the value of an independent and objective investigation grows. As Fujimoto puts it, "Companies need to think about whether a management-led investigation is worth the risk."

For example, would a management-led probe send the wrong signal? Would the fact that it was undertaken by in-house staff suggest a level of nonindependence that could undermine the results of the investigation? How would other interested parties, such as the external auditors, SEC, and Department of Justice, view the results of such an investigation?

Given the difficulty of these questions, it would seem wise to discuss them and incorporate the results into your fraud response plan before a serious fraud allegation occurs.

Establishing investigation protocols up front

One area where some companies have run into problems is with the way in which their investigations were conducted, which can adversely impact the credibility of the investigation, or lead to charges being made against the people and the company performing the investigation.

We sometimes describe investigations as being akin to performing a ballet in a minefield. They require very careful choreography. For example, overzealous investigators have at times misrepresented their identities to obtain private telephone records to which they were not entitled. Using experienced investigators can help to preserve the reputation of the company and those commissioning the investigation.

Interviews must be conducted in such a way as to avoid violations of laws, such as "false imprisonment" of interviewees. And any searches of employees' computers, desks or lockers need to comply with laws that protect employees' privacy.

The question of privacy expectations and legal standards is increasingly complex, especially for companies operating internationally in multiple jurisdictions. One approach is for a company to seek legal opinions to develop a roadmap of what can and cannot be done in the jurisdictions in which they do business, and to review the roadmap periodically.

Establishing investigation protocols governing how the investigation will be performed can help the company to achieve credibility for the investigation and reduce the risk of claims against the company arising from the investigation. These protocols can be established prior to each investigation, or, better still, be established by your legal counsel for use on all investigations. If your company does not have these in place already, now might be a good time to develop them.

Collecting and preserving crucial data

Another of our colleagues, Kevin Condon, notes that the most important first step in any investigation is preserving and collecting potentially relevant data as evidence. Most investigations begin in the accounting and finance departments, but important evidence can also be found in sales, warehousing, shipping, purchasing, IT, HR, and other key functional areas across the company.

Potentially relevant evidence can be found in both paper and electronic formats, including word processing documents, spreadsheets, presentations, ledgers, databases, and emails. By some accounts, electronic data today represents 97 percent of the information companies maintain. Fraud investigations reflect this statistic; they increasingly require sophisticated computer forensics and electronic evidence–handling capabilities, which are a specialty skill set.

Quick action can be essential to secure evidence, especially electronic evidence. People who commit fraud and corruption may seek to cover their trail by destroying evidence that might incriminate them. Prompt action by investigators increases the likelihood that this evidence can be secured from a backup file or recovered from deleted files that have not yet been overwritten. In addition, electronic evidence can be destroyed through day-to-day IT operations such as reusing backup tapes or automatically purging deleted files. Securing critical evidence and achieving a successful investigation may depend on having computer forensic capabilities ready to be deployed at a moment's notice.

"Many computer operating systems don't always work as people expect," according to our colleague, Bruce Hartley, an electronic discovery specialist. "They often don't really delete things; they may just remove pointers to things. Many times when we do a bit-for-bit copy of a hard drive and search for text strings we get all kinds of things that people don't realize are resident on their machines. People who may be committing fraud may have deleted their cache and sent messages using a personal email system or through instant messaging, but the contents may still in fact be traceable."

Take the necessary precautions to ensure that data is not corrupted, says Condon. Individuals with potentially relevant documents and other data would be instructed to safeguard them and not to modify or discard them. Investigators or lawyers working with computer forensic specialists then identify and collect the evidence in a manner that preserves its integrity and its admissibility in potential legal proceedings. Crucial to this task is that the investigation team is trained in evidence-handling and chain-of-custody issues. You do not want to find that your critical evidence is deemed inadmissible in court or, worse yet, corrupted or destroyed, because it was mishandled.

As the relevant documents are collected and analyzed, the investigation team will move ahead and begin conducting interviews. Typically, investigators start by identifying and interviewing the most junior witnesses and work their way up the corporate structure, building their understanding of the role of the most senior individuals. This process often reveals further evidence and witnesses, identifies additional links between people and relevant documents, and brings further pressure on those higher up who may have committed fraud or other malfeasance.

Newer challenges, newer technologies

Changes in corporate record keeping and document retention practices, whether undertaken in order to prepare for disasters or to comply with heightened regulations or enforcement and litigation requirements (e.g., electronic discovery obligations under the 2006 revisions to the Federal Rules of Civil Procedure), have led to new challenges and opportunities for corporate investigators facing exploding volumes of electronic data.

One challenge is that courts and regulators are becoming less sympathetic to companies that fail to preserve, locate, and produce responsive evidence from their electronically stored information

(ESI). The revised Federal Rules and those of many state equivalents, for example, place heightened obligations on litigants and potential litigants to prepare and provide data maps showing the location of all ESI in a company's active and archived computer systems.

The failure to comply with these obligations puts a company at a disadvantage vis-à-vis opposing parties who come to the "meet-and-confer" more prepared or government investigators who give credit for "cooperation." Conversely opportunity arises for those companies that are prepared at the "meet-and-confer" or who can "cooperate" with the government investigations.

Another challenge is the pervasiveness and complexity of certain ESI, especially email. Nearly everyone uses emails. Some employees have multiple accounts plus instant messaging, and such communications often grow into ongoing "threads" involving multiple recipients and numerous responses back and forth. Emails can be archived on the user's computer or on a network server. However, sometimes emails are automatically deleted through IT retention policies.

It is not difficult to imagine the challenges of having to identify potentially relevant ESI—emails, documents, spreadsheets, even voicemails—throughout a sprawling enterprise and at the individual personal computer (PC) level, preserving and collecting it both at a point in time and incrementally as information is added or modified. This challenge can be a costly and complicated undertaking for companies. It also poses distinct dangers if not carried out in a way that is compliant with the law. Courts increasingly are willing to impose sanctions on lawyers and companies for missteps in the electronic discovery process, and in some instances are effectively deciding the merits of the case based on the lack of fidelity to procedure.

Fortunately, newer technologies are being developed to help companies with these requirements. Especially promising are remote collection technologies. These technologies can be installed on every PC within a company and used to centrally search PCs for potentially relevant evidence, then collect it onto servers designed to preserve the evidence. Moreover, the search commands can be configured to remain on the PCs and collect any newly developed information that is potentially relevant and transfer it to the storage server. This process can be initiated whenever desired, such as upon notice of litigation, or when the company learns of a government investigation, or as part of an ongoing control to protect the company's assets from loss, misappropriation or misuse.

As technology improves, the challenges of ESI open new opportunities for investigators. Already the complexities of email preservation and review are mitigated by new tools to uncover fraud. Recently released software packages can track email communications graphically, giving an edge to investigators looking to discover who told what to whom and when. Other tools visually cluster emails by concepts, making it easier to focus on the suspect activity.

The day may soon come when investigators will be able to scour corporate computers for potentially relevant evidence, such as emails, collect and preserve it for legal compliance, and investigate the fraud, all remotely from a centralized location. Challenges of course remain in the form of PDAs, thumb drives, personal email accounts, personal server accounts, and other forms of non-corporate devices.

Communication—enough but not too much

It is important to maintain an open channel of communication among members of the investigation team so people understand the purpose of the process and their roles. But communications to others outside the team are generally tightly controlled to avoid prejudicing the investigation, inadvertently waiving legal privileges or leading to charges of defamation.

"Keep all interested parties informed on a timely basis," says Condon. "Make sure various parts of the team are communicating among each other and that updates are provided to the audit committee, external auditors, regulators, and management, as appropriate." Legal counsel leading the investigation typically manages the communication process to ensure that only appropriate information is shared.

The benefits of a case management system

It can be a challenge for senior management to keep tabs on the status of a single fraud investigation, especially if it spans multiple business units in the company and many different people. Now imagine a large multinational company that may deal with tens or hundreds of situations of potential wrongdoing of various kinds during the course of a year. Making sure each of those is handled appropriately and consistently can be extremely difficult.

Case management systems are increasingly used by leading companies to keep track of allegations received and the status of the company's actions to address the issue. The most sophisticated systems provide workflow capabilities to help companies assign follow-up tasks and direct them to the appropriate personnel while keeping track of the outstanding items. This functionality has the potential to enhance productivity while driving consistency and quality.

Some external providers of whistle-blower hotlines offer such case management systems and can feed new hotline reports directly into the system. They may also enable the company to enter into the system reports received through other means, such as those communicated directly to the legal function, human resources, compliance, ethics, fraud, security, customer service, internal audit, audit committee, board of directors, or to supervisors or managers in any part of the company.

When a case management system is used to track the resolution of allegations of wrongdoing, it can become a rich repository of information that can be used to enhance the company's fraud and corruption risk assessment process. It can provide data to measure the company's performance in resolving issues promptly or applying discipline consistently. In short, it can enable performance improvement.

Legal counsel may be involved in structuring the contents and use of the case management system so as to avoid breaches of legal privilege or confidentiality. Deploying case management tools can bring a new level of sophistication and management to the resolution of fraud, corruption, and other allegations in today's more complex companies.

Remediation—getting more value from investigations

Leading companies use fraud and corruption investigations not only to find out what happened but also to identify vulnerabilities in their core business processes weaknesses in their internal controls. Then they fix them, not only in the business unit where the issue arose but enterprise-wide. That way they can get more value out of fraud investigations and increase their fraud prevention capabilities.

This may seem like simple common sense, but too often companies fixate on putting out the immediate fire and do not take the time to better prevent future ones. Or they implement process and control improvements, but only in the business unit where the issue arose. Operating silos, communication challenges, or the lack of a collective antifraud culture can deter people from sharing insights that result from fraud investigations, leaving other parts of the company to learn them the hard way. That can be a costly way to operate.

As we stated above, what distinguishes more effective companies in this area, in our experience, is that they embrace, the opportunity to learn from incidents of fraud and corruption. They take the time to identify vulnerabilities in business processes and weaknesses in internal controls that permitted the wrongdoing to occur. They involve their internal auditors and other consultants in designing process and control improvements.

And they implement those improvements enterprise-wide. It is not rocket science; but it takes diligence and management support to make it happen. We believe that companies that employ these principles will be more resilient when confronted by fraud and corruption.

10

The Players' Roles (Including Yours)

Key points:

- ➤ The better you understand your business, the better prepared you might be to proactively manage fraud and corruption risks and deal with fraud when it occurs.
- ➤ Fraud and corruption risk management depends on close cooperation and coordination of the board, the audit committee, management, staff, and the internal audit function.
- ➤ Everyone in the company has a basic responsibility to help prevent and detect fraud and corruption. One of management's key roles is to educate and encourage employees to do this.
- ➤ The board and the audit committee play important roles in fraud and corruption risk management, providing oversight and a crucial check and balance on management.

New rules, new responsibilities

The first decade of the 21st century has been marked by a virtually unprecedented chain of developments in the realm of corporate governance. The public outcry that resulted in the Sarbanes-Oxley Act of 2002 and the ensuing implementation of that legislation brought a host of reforms and modifications to the financial reporting system. It may be fair to say that many companies are still sorting through those changes, and grappling with their various implications. The financial crisis of 2008 revealed additional issues related to the effectiveness of risk management in a variety of areas.

In most areas, the old rules still apply—the more thoroughly you know and understand your business, the better prepared you will be to deal with the challenges and obstacles that inevitably arise.

While this may seem obvious, a review of some of the more spectacular failures of the recent past shows that in many instances, top executives and boards appear not to have fully comprehended the risks in the businesses they were charged with running.

If you do not understand the business itself, it is virtually impossible to understand the risks associated with the business. So, the first rule of managing fraud and corruption risks is: *Know your business.*

But there are enough new rules to justify a review of how the corporate governance landscape has changed since 2002, even noting that it will likely undergo still more change as a result of the sub-prime mortgage issue and the ensuing financial crisis of 2008.

While the impact of Sarbanes-Oxley has been significant, it is important to remember that it was only one component of a broader effort to restore public confidence in the capital markets. In a February 2002 speech by Harvey Pitt, then chairman of the Securities and Exchange Commission (SEC), Pitt asked that national self-regulatory organizations (SROs), such as the New York Stock Exchange (NYSE) and NASDAQ, critically review their listing standards and propose modifications to enhance the corporate governance of listed companies.

As a result, the NYSE and NASDAQ separately developed proposals for new corporate governance rules and submitted them to the SEC for consideration. After reviewing public comments and various amendments submitted by the SROs, the SEC approved the new corporate governance listing standards on November 4, 2003.

The new standards of the NYSE and NASDAQ include a range of requirements affecting boards of directors, certain board committees, and management. For instance, both sets of standards:

- Require that a majority of the board be composed of independent directors

- Strengthen the criteria for an independent director determination
- Place responsibility for director nominations and executive compensation in the hands of the independent directors
- Require separate meetings for non-management or independent board members
- Require a code of business conduct/ethics for all directors, officers, and employees

Among other provisions, the NYSE standards required companies to establish and disclose corporate governance guidelines that address specified criteria; the NASDAQ standards required companies to make a public announcement if they receive an audit opinion with a going-concern emphasis.

In addition to the various general governance practices covered, the new listing standards modified a number of audit committee requirements, including composition criteria and responsibilities.

The NYSE standards are more detailed than the NASDAQ standards in specifying the audit committee's responsibilities. Many of the responsibilities specified in the NYSE standards, but not specified in the NASDAQ standards, have become common practice for a number of public companies, regardless of where they are listed.

In any event, it is absolutely crucial for top management to possess a broad understanding of the roles and responsibilities of the different players involved in a strong fraud and corruption risk management strategy.

In our view, fraud and corruption risk management depends on close cooperation and coordination of the board, the audit committee, management, staff, and the internal audit function. It is essential for everyone to have a basic grasp of who is responsible for doing what.

There is another important point to make about who the players are in managing fraud and corruption risks. Not only is it vital to recognize that virtually the entire company must be involved in some way, it is also important to note the issues concerning formalization of roles and responsibilities. *Managing the Business Risk of Fraud: A Practical Guide* clearly makes this point:

> To help ensure an organization's fraud risk management program [is] effective, it is important to understand the roles and

responsibilities that personnel at all levels of the organization have with respect to fraud risk management. Policies, job descriptions, charters, and/or delegations of authority should define roles and responsibilities related to fraud risk management. In particular, the documentation should articulate who is responsible for the governance oversight of fraud control (i.e., the role and responsibility of the board of directors and/or designated committee of the board). Documentation should also reflect management's responsibility for the design and implementation of the fraud risk strategy, and how different segments of the organization support fraud risk management.

The board of directors and audit committee

Under the new listing rules, the audit committee of the board has emerged as a crucial point of connection between the various levels and areas of the company responsible for managing fraud risks. In addition to overseeing the company's financial reporting processes and internal controls, the audit committee serves as the interface between the company and its external auditor.

The board's and audit committee's roles and responsibilities relating to fraud and corruption risk management generally include:

- Setting the right tone at the top
- Understanding what constitutes fraud and corruption risk
- Appropriately involving those charged with governance in an oversight capacity
- Conducting its own brainstorming discussion, including a specific discussion about how senior management might attempt to override existing controls
- Reviewing and approving management's fraud and corruption risk assessment
- Overseeing the whistle-blower program and enforcement by management of the code of conduct
- Evaluating management's effectiveness in establishing fraud controls in light of any identified deficiencies
- Reporting violations, including fraud, to regulatory agencies

Management

Ultimately management is responsible for implementing and supporting the policies and procedures designed to mitigate fraud and corruption risks and safeguard the assets of the company. Management is also responsible for making certain that the controls and processes for mitigating risk are up to date and functioning properly.

Additionally, of course, management is responsible for the company's financial statements. For SEC registrants, the CEO and CFO are required to certify the company's financial statements, underscoring their fiduciary and personal responsibilities.

Management's roles and responsibilities relating to fraud risk management generally include:

- Performing a periodic fraud and corruption risk assessment
- Establishing and maintaining fraud controls
- Maintaining adequate documentation of design of fraud controls
- Evaluating design and operating effectiveness of fraud controls
- Evaluating and communicating fraud control deficiencies
- Educating the employees on ethics and fraud
- Setting and modeling the right ethical tone for the company
- Enforcing the code of conduct

Some executives and other managers in a company may be reluctant to accept these responsibilities, perhaps thinking that it's not their job. How can they be persuaded that it is important to the company that they do this and do it well? Gavin Ingram is Corporate Counsel Asia for BlueScope Steel Limited, the leading steel company in Australia and New Zealand with operations in Asia and the United States. According to Gavin, "It comes back to the culture of the organization. I draw a parallel with our safety culture. Above all else we value the safety of our employees and aiming for zero harm is our number one priority. Everyone in the organization has a part to play in making our employees feel safe and we believe it is the same with business conduct. We make it very clear that business conduct is everyone's responsibility."

There are several functions that can perform parts of management's roles and responsibilities. For example, Compliance and/or

Legal could be responsible for enforcing the code of conduct, educating the employees on ethics and fraud, and working with the CEO/Chairman to set and model the right ethical tone for the company. The risk management function could be responsible for facilitating the fraud and corruption risk assessment, with involvement from various functions across the company. Finance and accounting, with assistance from Internal Audit, may be responsible for evaluating the design and operating effectiveness of financial controls and communicating deficiencies.

A wide array of functions would typically establish and maintain the fraud controls, including finance and accounting, information technology, human resources, compliance, legal, security, and loss prevention.

If there was previously any doubt about responsibilities for anti-fraud controls, the Sarbanes-Oxley Act of 2002 made things more certain. Let us begin by looking at some of the requirements for SEC registrants.

Section 404 of the Sarbanes-Oxley Act of 2002, *Management Assessment of Internal Controls,* requires company management to file an annual report on internal control over financial reporting.

The SEC's resultant *Final Rule: Management's Reports on Internal Control Over Financial Reporting and Certification of Disclosure in Exchange Act Periodic Reports* provides guidance on management's responsibilities related to fraud:

> The assessment of a company's internal control over financial reporting must be based on procedures sufficient both to evaluate its design and to test its operating effectiveness. Controls subject to such assessment include . . . controls related to the prevention, identification, and detection of fraud. (see footnote 2)

The SEC's Sarbanes-Oxley section 404 guidance to management that was released August 2007 emphasizes the importance of anti-fraud programs and controls in a company's internal controls over the financial reporting process. This guidance states:

> Management's evaluation of the risk of misstatement should include consideration of the vulnerability of the entity to

fraudulent activity (for example, fraudulent financial reporting, misappropriation of assets and corruption), and whether
any such exposure could result in a material misstatement of
the financial statements.

Management should recognize that the risk of material
misstatement due to fraud ordinarily exists in any organization,
regardless of size or type, and it may vary by specific location
or segment and by individual financial reporting element. For
example, one type of fraud risk that has resulted in fraudulent
financial reporting in companies of all sizes and types is the
risk of improper override of internal controls in the financial
reporting process. While the identification of a fraud risk is not
necessarily an indication that a fraud has occurred, the absence
of an identified fraud is not an indication that no fraud risks
exist. Rather, these risk assessments are used in evaluating
whether adequate controls have been implemented.

Our discussion of fraud and corruption risk assessment in
Chapter 5 illustrates the operational challenges that can be encoun-
tered when implementing this guidance, especially around the issue
of management override of internal controls. Noting these issues in
advance can help you to address them up front and produce a better result.

Staff

It is not an exaggeration to say that in today's business environment, more is expected of everyone. As corporate hierarchies flat-
ten, personal responsibility becomes more important at every level.
As such, every employee has become a potentially valuable player in
a company's fraud and corruption risk management strategy.

Staff's roles and responsibilities relating to fraud and corruption risk management generally include:

- Understanding their role in managing fraud and corruption
  risks
- Reading and understanding policies and procedures
- Participating in the process of creating a strong control
  environment

- Business process owner's involvement in fraud and corruption risk brainstorming
- Being aware of red flags
- Reporting incidences of potential fraud and corruption

We noted previously the key role that tips can play in detecting fraud schemes and corruption, and the requirement for SEC registrants to deploy confidential reporting mechanisms such as hotlines. We also noted the difficulties in resisting management overrides of controls. In both areas, the most important variable is whether the staff believe in the company's repudiation of fraud and corruption and has incorporated that psychological stance into their everyday corporate behavior.

The workforce itself clearly plays a fundamentally important role as guardian and watchdog. For employees to play this crucial role, however, they must be comfortable using hotlines and comfortable resisting attempts to go around controls. Developing that comfort level starts with the tone at the top of the company, but it extends into many features of the relationship of the staff to the company, from compensation policies, to rewards for transparency, to performance evaluation.

Internal audit

In many companies, the internal audit function reports directly and primarily to the audit committee, giving it a higher degree of independence from management than it had in the past. With greater independence, however, comes heightened responsibility. Internal audit is expected to communicate swiftly with the audit committee particularly when there are significant deviations from policies or procedures, or when there is a major breakdown in controls.

Internal audit's roles and responsibilities relating to fraud and corruption risk management generally include:

- Supporting management's education of personnel regarding ethics, fraud, and corruption
- Assisting in the evaluation of fraud risk factors, fraud and corruption risks, and schemes
- Assisting in the development of fraud controls based on its understanding of operations and internal audit findings

- Monitoring for compliance, including interrogation of databases and applications
- Supporting the audit committee by performing proactive fraud auditing to address the risk of management override of controls
- Performing proactive monitoring of various aspects of the fraud and corruption risk management program

Of course, this implies that internal audit has appropriate staffing and funding. The appropriate role of internal audit can be stifled in more ways than one. In the case of the United Nations and the Oil-for-Food Programme abuses, for example, the Independent Inquiry Committee led by Paul Volcker found that the internal audit function was compromised not only by program management interference, but also by severe shortfalls in staffing and budget restraints. The net result was that internal audit was not able to conduct examinations in Iraq, the main site of abuses, and was not therefore able to detect the rampant corruption that occurred.

Interestingly, the example of internal audit and the Oil-for-Food Programme also raises a fundamental question of competency and the way budget restraints can hamper the development of appropriate competencies. We have stressed the importance of corruption risk assessments. At a time when the United Nations was attempting to move to risk based audits, the internal auditors asked for funds to engage a consultant to help them develop additional competency for use in the Oil-for-Food audits. The request was denied by the program management executive. In hindsight, Mr. Volcker's committee found that a competent risk assessment of the program had never been carried out.

Independent auditors

The role of independent auditors is described in Statement on Auditing Standards (SAS) No. 1, *Codification of Auditing Standards and Procedures* (AICPA, *Professional Standards*, vol. 1, AU section 110, "Responsibilities and Functions of the Independent Auditor"), which states:

> The objective of the ordinary audit of financial statements by the independent auditor is the expression of an opinion on the fairness with which they present, in all material respects, financial position, results of operations, and its cash flows in conformity with generally accepted accounting principles.

AU section 110 also states:

> The auditor has a responsibility to plan and perform the audit to obtain reasonable assurance about whether the financial statements are free of material misstatement, whether caused by error or fraud.

AU section 316, "Consideration of Fraud in a Financial Statement Audit," establishes standards and provides guidance to auditors in fulfilling that responsibility, as it relates to fraud, in an audit of financial statements conducted in accordance with generally accepted auditing standards.

Reporting on internal controls is not currently part of most financial statement audits, such as those of private or smaller public companies. Currently, some large public companies are required under section 404 of the Sarbanes-Oxley Act to have their independent auditors audit and report on management's assessment of internal control over financial reporting. Internal control over financial reporting encompasses certain fraud controls.

The standard governing the independent auditor's evaluation of internal controls over financial reporting is issued by the Public Company Accounting Oversight Board. It is Auditing Standard No. 5 and it states:

> . . . the risk that a company's internal control over financial reporting will fail to prevent or detect misstatement caused by fraud usually is higher than the risk of failure to prevent or detect error. The auditor should focus more of his or her attention on the areas of highest risk.

This Standard also states:

> When planning and performing the audit of internal control over financial reporting, the auditor should take into account the results of his or her fraud risk assessment. As part of identifying and testing entity-level controls, as discussed beginning at paragraph 22, and selecting other controls to test, as discussed beginning at paragraph 39, the auditor should evaluate whether the company's controls sufficiently address identified risks of material misstatement due to fraud and controls intended to address the risk of management override of other controls.

These requirements are currently only applicable to certain large public companies ("accelerated filers"). It remains to be seen if these additional measures that help to address the risk of fraud will be implemented for smaller public companies as well. Implementation has been deferred by regulators several times and continues to be the subject of public debate.

Other consultants

Management and the Board should also consider calling on outside consultants to assist in the development of fraud and corruption risk management programs. Such consultants often have substantial knowledge not only regarding what is possible in fraud and corruption risk management, but also about particular controls and industry benchmarking that can be essential to balancing and tuning controls to the risks that are dominant in the industry.

In this book, we have stressed the pivotal role of the fraud and corruption risk assessment and of the controls that follow from it. We argue that these things, if done correctly, can lead to corporate resiliency. However, as important as they are, we should not assume that all companies are fully equipped to carry them out.

Most companies, even large complex ones, are designed to carry out business functions related to commercial transactions. As such, they may require some form of assistance in developing fraud and corruption risk management capabilities and programs, which can also involve elements of change management.

This is especially the case with fraud and corruption risk assessments, which, as Chapter 5 makes clear, present many traps for the unwary. Leveraging assistance from outside the company can make a lot of sense.

The value of a cross-functional committee

Fraud and corruption risk management is not just the responsibility of one department. It requires collaboration between people in different functions such as finance and accounting, internal audit, information technology, human resources, fraud/security, compliance, legal, and risk management. In the real world, this can sometimes mean dealing with silos, turf issues, and empires, which can hamper company-wide efforts to combat fraud and corruption.

A cross-functional fraud and corruption risk management committee representing various functions can help overcome the obstacles posed by silos and enable a fraud and corruption risk management strategy that is genuinely effective at multiple levels and in multiple areas of the company.

Such a committee can include representatives from the key business functions identified above. Ideally, the committee can meet regularly to discuss their various tasks, share knowledge, and foster a sense of teamwork.

It is important to assign one person or function as the project manager to manage and facilitate the different tasks of this committee, in addition to a chairperson to ensure that roles and responsibilities are properly designed and that the fraud and corruption risk management strategy is properly implemented.

The role of the compliance officer

Back in Chapter 5, we discussed the role of senior management in setting the proper tone to establish an effective control environment. A company's compliance officer also plays a critical role in setting the right tone for compliance. If the tone set by the compliance officer is overly rigid, preachy, or authoritarian, people might become too reluctant or too fearful to report suspected occurrences of fraud or corruption.

The tone set by the compliance officer can also affect business operations across the entity. If the company's compliance processes are perceived as fair and rational, they are less likely to impede the normal flow of business. If, on the other hand, they are perceived as harsh and unreasonable, they might actually prevent people from embracing normal and reasonable risks that are inherent in many business activities.

"Compliance officers form the bridge between the worlds of legal risk and business performance," says our colleague Steve Vincze. "They need to understand the business so they can make sure that the compliance operations are integrated with the business operations."

A former compliance officer in the life sciences industry, Vincze has seen the role transform over time. "Historically, compliance has been a reactive function. But that is changing. Nowadays, the compliance officer is a team player. You have got to be collaborative, energetic, and knowledgeable. You need to resonate with credibility across all levels. You need to have an extraordinarily positive outlook."

To a greater extent than before, today's compliance officer is expected to stay ahead of the curve by understanding the complex and continually evolving relationships among business, risk, and regulation.

Ideally, the compliance officer is perceived as a business resource instead of an adversary. "Good compliance officers distill very complicated requirements into simple concepts that people can understand and act upon with confidence. A good compliance program is ready to answer the question that has never been asked," says Vincze.

Compliance officers are more likely to be effective, says Vincze, when they view compliance as an integrated business process, rather than as a mandated "bolt on" that people might tend to resent.

"You need to show people that you are adding value and making a difference in a positive way," says Vincze. "Ironically, you have got to take some risks to do the job right."

Fraud and corruption risk management is everyone's business

We have argued in this chapter that managing fraud and corruption risk is not the business of "this or that" group within a company. Instead, it is everyone's business, from clerks in the accounting department, to company management, to the audit committee of the board of directors. *Managing the Business Risk of Fraud: A Practical Guide* sums up this concept:

> Reactions to recent corporate scandals have led the public and stakeholders to expect organizations to take a "no fraud tolerance" attitude. Good governance principles demand that an organization's board of directors, or equivalent oversight body, ensure overall high ethical behavior in the organization, regardless of its status as public, private, government, or not-for-profit; its relative size; or its industry. The board's role is critically important because historically most major frauds are perpetrated by senior management in collusion with other employees. Vigilant handling of fraud cases within an organization sends clear signals to the public, stakeholders, and

regulators about the board and management's attitude toward fraud risks and about the organization's fraud risk tolerance.

Fraud and corruption may be tougher to manage than some other risks, in part because it can involve getting many different functions within the company to work together effectively. But when that happens, duplicative activities can be negotiated away, gaps can be identified and closed, and fraud and corruption risk management performance can be raised. Fraud and corruption risk management is everyone's job in a company. And it is a great thing to see when people embrace the opportunity to help create a workplace that has more integrity, less fraud and corruption, and more effective risk management.

Conclusion: What the Future May Hold

We hope that by now we have made a strong case for building a more proactive and more focused approach to managing fraud and corruption risks across your company and for the way in which such an approach can lead to increased corporate resiliency.

We have striven to present a strong argument in favor of proactive anti-fraud and anti-corruption strategies. We believe such strategies are attractive to reduce the likelihood of fraud and corruption occurring and to reduce the impact on the entity when they do.

In our experience, companies that prepare for the eventuality of fraud and corruption do a better job of coping and recovering than companies that wait until something unfortunate has occurred. Formulating a response to fraud after it has occurred is like closing the proverbial barn door after the horses have escaped. It is sometimes too late.

Sadly, we have personally witnessed numerous occasions in which companies have acted to address fraud risks only after embarrassing revelations, extensive investigations, and costly legal proceedings have occurred. We have seen too many companies wait until after they have been publicly humiliated, had their reputations tarnished, and lost substantial market value before taking what we consider to be prudent steps to manage fraud risks.

We urge you to consider taking action before the storm hits. Be prepared. Do not wait until circumstances force you into a reactive mode. The processes and techniques for managing fraud and corruption risks proactively exist. Take the time to learn more about them. Make the commitment to consider their relative merits and advantages. Then act decisively to develop and implement a strong fraud and corruption risk management strategy.

We obviously cannot guarantee that taking these steps will result in your experiencing no fraud or corruption, or protect you entirely from their effects. But we can state that from our experience you will likely avoid some frauds and be better positioned to recover more quickly when some inevitably occur. You will also likely be in a better position to limit the extent of the damage.

On a cautionary note, it seems reasonably fair to point out that, based on the periodicity of previous business cycles, we appear to be in another patch of relatively stormy weather. In other words, batten down the hatches.

Why do we say this? Based on our personal experience and observations, periods marked by economic turmoil, as in the case of the current financial crisis and recession, are commonly accompanied by revelations of rampant episodes of fraud and corruption (some committed during boom times, some during the subsequent downturn). These periods are usually followed by times marked by closer scrutiny, heightened regulation, and sterner punishments. After that comes a period of relative calm during which people may in time grow complacent and somewhat lax, thereby allowing more fraud and corruption to be committed. And then the cycle starts again.

Whether you accept the inevitability of certain business cycles or not, you cannot casually accept the inevitability of fraud and corruption. That would be wrong, and imprudent. It would also be bad for business, since as we have maintained throughout this book, resilient companies, those that do a good job of managing fraud risks, may gain competitive advantages over companies that do not.

Additionally, one can argue that in today's global economy, many companies have more to lose than ever before. Their global value chains now expose them to more fraud and corruption risks from countries far away. Mergers have led to much larger companies with more shareholder value dependent on intangibles like brand names and reputation. But the global media now brings corporate misfeasance anywhere in the world to the public's attention, increasing the risk of reputational loss. And prosecutors and regulators in more countries are aggressively enforcing the growing array of anti-fraud and anti-corruption laws. We believe all these factors can make companies more brittle and therefore more vulnerable than companies of the past.

All this is before factoring in the impact of the ongoing global recession and corporate financing challenges. The current shortage of debtor-in-possession financing, for example, is turning Chapter 11 bankruptcy from a restructuring opportunity into a forced liquidation for more companies. Companies that experience major fraud or corruption and which in the past might have used Chapter 11 to help them recover may now have greater difficulty surviving.

Resilient corporations understand that strong fraud and corruption risk management strategies can help them become more flexible and more capable of surviving the next storm.

Today's business environment clearly requires a greater emphasis on effective risk management generally than was considered necessary in the past. Does it not make sense to manage fraud risks better too?

"Look, most Western nations have foreign corrupt practices legislation. The more you expand globally, the more you increase your exposure to the risk of prosecution for fraud and corruption, especially when you're operating in countries that rank higher on Transparency International's Corruption Perceptions Index," says Peter Dent, a Deloitte Canada colleague and a former fraud and corruption investigator at the World Bank.

"Prevention is always cheaper than the cure. But it's hard convincing people to invest in fraud prevention because they just can't envision the risks," says Dent. "So we're still seeing people enacting preventive strategies after the fact, when they're overwhelmed by their circumstances and the damage has already been done."

Dent, who spent much of his time with the World Bank investigating fraud and corruption in Southeast Asia, says the inability of executives to comprehend the enormous downside risk of fraud remains a problem. "There are huge risks and the costs are astronomical. But nobody wants to think negatively about the future. Many people still believe that planning for fraud is like planning for a funeral. But when the prosecutors start knocking at the door, you're more likely to survive the crisis if you've already taken the right steps."

Good fraud and corruption risk assessment is crucial

Once we accept the proposition that companies that develop fraud risk strategies are more likely to be successful than those that do not, we must turn to the key area of potential vulnerability, fraud and corruption risk assessment. We believe that many companies fall short in this area and would be better off if they were more methodical in identifying the fraud and corruption risks they face and coupling the risks to appropriate strategies.

More frequent, more skeptical, and more thorough fraud and corruption risk assessments are a crucial defensive strategy. The reason, of course, is simple: If you do not know what is out there waiting for you, you cannot hope to prepare for it. Yesterday's tactics will not help you cope with the fraud risks of today and tomorrow. Honesty, candor, and thoroughness are prerequisites for a fraud and corruption risk assessment strategy, especially when you consider how quickly new risks can emerge.

One of the goals here is avoiding surprises. The more you know about the risks you are facing, the less likely you are to be caught "wrong-footed." So, in addition to identifying fraud and corruption risks more frequently and more methodically, you should also be realistic about your company's capabilities.

Companies rarely have all the resources at their disposal necessary to solve or mitigate every conceivable fraud risk. Resilient corporations are not afraid to leverage external resources to acquire the knowledge, experience, or capabilities they need to strengthen their anti-fraud strategies. That may, of course, seem self-serving for advisors to say, but in practice we see many companies that have fallen behind in their approach to fraud and corruption risk management and an external perspective can be valuable.

Resilient corporations resist the urge to rely on internal "groupthink" when confronted with potential risks. Sometimes trying to solve a problem by relying solely on internal resources can misfire. Consider reaching out to advisors that can help or assist you in finding the information you need or develop the capabilities required to solve the problem.

Embracing new roles and responsibilities

Resilient corporations we have worked with embrace the newer, more substantive relationship between the board and the audit committee. This relationship is a key difference between the pre– and post– Sarbanes-Oxley era. Ideally, it can lead to greater strength and greater resiliency for companies competing in complex, fast-changing global markets.

The role of the corporate officer designated by the chief executive to be responsible for fraud and corruption risk management will be increasingly important in coordinating the entity's activities across multiple functions and operating units. Healthy interrelationships among the board, the audit committee, and the individuals tasked with assessing risks and managing them appropriately are a crucial part of an ongoing enterprise-wide fraud and corruption risk management strategy.

Measuring performance

It would be foolish to suggest that you could manage your fraud and corruption risks properly without first having the willingness and the capability to monitor, test, and measure the effectiveness of your anti-fraud processes.

Resilient corporations emphasize performance testing and measurement and integrate them into their anti-fraud strategies. They establish key performance indicators (KPIs), measure progress and performance, produce reports on a periodic basis, share critical data with the board and the audit committee, strive to accomplish targets set by management with the board's approval, take corrective action when necessary, and drive toward continuous improvement.

In other words, they treat fraud and corruption risk management as an integral part of the business, not as an afterthought.

We won't predict the future, but . . .

Predicting what is going to happen next in the world of fraud and corruption is like predicting the weather — possible, but still subject to many uncertainties.

With that caveat in mind, we thought it would be useful to share some general perceptions held by our colleagues and clients regarding possible areas in which fraud and corruption challenges might arise with greater frequency and potentially heavier impact.

Our colleague Greg Swinehart, national leader of the Forensic and Dispute Services practice at Deloitte Financial Advisory Services LLP, identifies four trends that he believes are likely to exert a strong influence on the course of anti-fraud and anti-corruption efforts over the next several years:

1. **Globalization.** As companies engage with more markets around the world, the challenges of dealing with divergent accounting systems, different regulatory environments, and varying degrees of transparency will become greater. "Every cliché about the world becoming flat is true," says Swinehart. "Handling global investigations, managing anti-fraud programs in a global scale — the challenges are getting bigger, not smaller."

2. **Changes in regulatory regimes.** The worldwide financial problems are likely to result in regulatory changes in the United States and other countries. "We have had an incrementally changing regulatory environment for the past several years, but I think given what is happening in the global financial markets, we are likely to see accelerating change," says our colleague.

3. **Economic pressures.** The global recession may create intense economic pressures for an extended period, according to our colleague. "We know from our past experience that as the economic waters recede, more rocks are exposed. The real question is whether companies will mitigate the growing pressure on their people and help them avoid being tempted to resort to fraud and corruption," says Swinehart.

4. **Technology.** As companies rely more extensively on advanced technologies to operate their businesses, new opportunities for committing fraud will arise. "Every time that the guys with the white hats get better at devising anti-fraud systems — anomaly detection systems, control systems, security systems, firewalls and anti-penetration techniques — technologically savvy fraudsters, whether they are external to the company or internal, figure out a way around the technology. This battle will become more intense and it is likely to be with us for the rest of our lives."

Take your first steps now

Now that you are almost finished reading our book, we urge you to revisit Chapter 4 and take another look at the self-assessment tool. Take some time to answer the questions and then see where your company may be on the corporate resiliency scale with respect to managing fraud and corruption risks.

Chances are that you will find some indications that your company has an opportunity to make significant improvements. Resolve to take action as expeditiously as possible. Set a bar for yourself and see how much further you can drive your company up the scale. Remember that your specific areas of opportunity will likely include items beyond those covered in the self-assessment tool; it is simply a sample of questions intended to take your temperature on the issue of corporate resiliency.

For more information about fraud, corruption and other complex business issues, we encourage you to visit us at the Deloitte Forensic Center online at www.deloitte.com/us/forensiccenter.

We wish you the best of luck, and we wish you a resilient future.

Afterword

What are the best words to describe today's business environment? Complex? Volatile? Challenging? Uncertain?

One thing is clear: The values and integrity of individuals and the companies to which they belong are being tested to an unprecedented degree.

Our global economy is a new economy. It is a frontier, and we are all pioneers. We are inspired, we are awed, and we are more than occasionally confused by what we see happening around us.

In the midst of this uncertainty, we rightly look for standards of proper behavior to guide us. We know that honesty and integrity are still important and that even in the most competitive circumstances, the ability to behave ethically remains paramount.

That is why I am pleased that Toby and Frank devoted an entire chapter of this book to the crucial role of tone at the top and establishing an effective control environment.

If you believe, as I do, that a control environment is perhaps the single most important element of a company's anti-fraud strategy, then you will probably agree that one of management's most important responsibilities is setting the proper tone and making certain that it becomes the prime motivating principle at every level within the company.

This is not solely the job of the CEO. All of senior management should be involved. The board of directors, the audit committee, and internal audit also play key roles in setting the tone and culture of the company.

An effective control environment reduces the chances that employees will commit fraud. It clearly communicates a zero-tolerance attitude toward any and all types of fraud. It rejects corruption unambiguously.

In my experience as a CEO and as an anti-fraud, anti-corruption investigator and consultant, I have seen that a strong and unmistakable message from senior management can result in a better work environment that attracts better job candidates, encourages employee retention, and reduces unnecessary turnover.

At the risk of repeating some of the points made in this book, there are many ways for senior management to go about the task of setting the right tone. But the basic steps are straightforward and relatively easy to convey, if not to accomplish:

1. Management communicates what it expects of employees.
2. Management leads by example.
3. Management provides a safe, usable mechanism for reporting violations.
4. Management rewards integrity and ethical behavior.

As you can see, this is not rocket science. However, it is not completely intuitive, either, particularly in our challenging times. We are not necessarily born with the skills and abilities required to become effective and ethical leaders — that is why management books such as *Corporate Resiliency* are so useful.

Successful leaders learn that promoting ethical behavior and personal integrity is, above all, a team effort. Once the tone has been set, everyone in the company is responsible for making sure it is applied consistently. That is the hallmark of a truly ethical company. It is not just honest and ethical in some areas; it is honest and ethical everywhere it operates.

This concept of a code of conduct may be new to many companies, especially if they have not operated in a global marketplace before. But as Toby and Frank point out, it has become a necessary concept. A quick glance at the headlines will show you that prosecutions for alleged violations of the Foreign Corrupt Practices Act have risen dramatically.

Foreign governments that might have ignored corruption previously are now increasingly taking it more seriously, and are actively participating in efforts to chase down violators. Stiff fines and prison sentences are becoming increasingly common. The reputational damages resulting from prosecution are difficult to quantify, but it is hard to imagine that any company can benefit from having one or more of its officers in jail.

Companies all over the world have grappled with the challenges of fraud and corruption. But in many instances, and for a variety of reasons, these challenges did not receive the attention they fully deserved.

As a result, some companies never took the trouble to develop comprehensive strategies for managing fraud risks intelligently over time. Instead they settled for ad hoc mixtures of disparate tactical processes. Sometimes these makeshift approaches worked, and sometimes they did not. We have all seen the results that sometimes followed.

In today's business environment, fraud can no longer be considered a secondary concern. Smart companies are likely to perceive fraud as a primary risk. They understand that fraud is like a game of Russian roulette — even if the odds of surviving are in your favor, the downside can be especially ugly.

They also understand that the phenomenon of fraud has changed. In times past, a series of natural barriers normally prevented the effects of fraud from rippling too far beyond the boundaries of an individual business unit or operational area within a larger company.

In today's highly communication-efficient world, many of those barriers no longer exist. Modern companies tend to be flat, lean, and decentralized. The speed of business, the emphasis on productivity, and the relentless drive toward greater efficiency have brought new wealth and prosperity to millions of people worldwide. Moreover, analysts today move quickly and efficiently. Business advances and communication have opened the doors to new risks.

In our rapidly evolving global economy, fraud can come from any direction, at any time. New forms of fraud emerge at a dizzying pace, requiring companies to respond more quickly and with far greater flexibility than in the past.

The sheer volume of data that companies must process, screen, sort, and protect requires a new generation of more powerful tools that can address fraud risks in real time, before they spiral out of control.

Today, the Internet and other new media virtually guarantee that bad news will spread globally, amplifying risks and creating new ones. Fraud and corruption now have greater potential to ignite a chain reaction of events that could result in catastrophe.

In this book, Toby and Frank build a case for replacing short-term tactical approaches with sustainable strategies for managing fraud risks. They argue that resilient corporations do not wait for fraud to occur. Resilient corporations know that fraud and corruption may occur, so they develop and deploy effective strategies for preventing, detecting and responding to them.

The key is preparedness, and preparedness comes in two flavors: operational and cultural.

Operational preparedness includes all the people, processes and technologies required to sustain an effective anti-fraud strategy. Of the two kinds of preparedness, it's the easier to achieve.

Cultural preparedness is a little more difficult, since it requires a continual focus on managing fraud risks across the entire company.

As I suggested earlier, cultural preparedness begins with the tone at the top. It radiates in all directions, informing every decision made at every level and in every area of the company. It even extends beyond the traditional limits of the company, since it also must inform the decisions of business partners, suppliers, agents, and customers.

I would also like to make another point this book makes. As I have said in many speeches and interviews, and as I have made sure my company tries to live, innovation and new uses of technology are key issues in the fight against fraud and corruption. Things like a focus on the psychology of fraud and testing procedures to help identify prospective employees whose personality shows a propensity to commit fraud, as well as things like the continuous monitoring of financial transactions to screen for those that raise red flags, are examples of steps that companies should explore and be prepared to take.

From my perspective, a resilient corporation is a company that is both operationally and culturally prepared to manage fraud risks on a 24/7 basis, throughout the company. And I pose this question to you: Is your company prepared? Is it resilient?

Resiliency is not some kind of management-speak buzzword used by consultants. Resiliency is the ability to bounce back and regain your form after a shock. It is that simple. So, I ask you again: Is your company resilient? When something bad happens, how quickly and how completely will it recover?

I would not press the point if I did not believe wholeheartedly that resiliency is both an achievable and a necessary goal. Resiliency is a critical corporate asset. In fact, I would be willing to argue that resiliency, as defined in this excellent book by Toby and Frank, should be considered a core competency of successful companies.

By Frank Piantidosi
Chief Executive Officer, Deloitte North American Financial Advisory LLC

Appendix: Examples of Fraud Risk Factors

The following examples of fraud risk factors may be helpful to directors, officers, executives, and managers for brainstorming fraud risks at their organization and maintaining vigilance for indicators of potential fraud risks. Chapter 5, Fraud and Corruption Risk Assessment, describes how identification of fraud risk factors fits into the overall fraud risk assessment process.

This material is based on U.S. Auditing Standards AU316. Copyright 2002 by the American Institute of Certified Public Accountants, Inc. Adapted with permission.

Risk factors relating to misstatements arising from fraudulent financial reporting

The following are examples of risk factors relating to misstatements arising from fraudulent financial reporting.

Incentives/pressures

   a. Financial stability or profitability is threatened by economic, industry, or entity operating conditions, such as (or as indicated by):
- High degree of competition or market saturation, accompanied by declining margins
- High vulnerability to rapid changes, such as changes in technology, product obsolescence, or interest rates
- Significant declines in customer demand and increasing business failures in either the industry or overall economy

- Operating losses making the threat of bankruptcy, foreclosure, or hostile takeover imminent
- Recurring negative cash flows from operations or an inability to generate cash flows from operations while reporting earnings and earnings growth
- Rapid growth or unusual profitability, especially compared to that of other companies in the same industry
- New accounting, statutory, or regulatory requirements

b. Excessive pressure exists for management to meet the requirements or expectations of third parties due to the following:

- Profitability or trend level expectations of investment analysts, institutional investors, significant creditors, or other external parties (particularly expectations that are unduly aggressive or unrealistic), including expectations created by management in, for example, overly optimistic press releases or annual report messages
- Need to obtain additional debt or equity financing to stay competitive—including financing of major research and development or capital expenditures
- Marginal ability to meet exchange listing requirements or debt repayment or other debt covenant requirements
- Perceived or real adverse effects of reporting poor financial results on significant pending transactions, such as business combinations or contract awards

c. Information available indicates that the personal financial situation of the management or those charged with governance is threatened by the entity's financial performance arising from the following:

- Significant financial interests in the entity
- Significant portions of their compensation (for example, bonuses, stock options, and earn-out arrangements) being contingent upon achieving aggressive targets for stock price, operating results, financial position, or cash flow
- Personal guarantees of debts of the entity

d. There is excessive pressure on management or operating personnel to meet financial targets set up by those charged with governance, including sales or profitability incentive goals.

Opportunities

a. The nature of the industry or the entity's operations provides opportunities to engage in fraudulent financial reporting that can arise from the following:
  - Significant related-party transactions not in the ordinary course of business or with related entities not audited or audited by another firm
  - A strong financial presence or ability to dominate a certain industry sector that allows the entity to dictate terms or conditions to suppliers or customers that may result in inappropriate or non-arm's-length transactions
  - Assets, liabilities, revenues, or expenses based on significant estimates that involve subjective judgments or uncertainties that are difficult to corroborate
  - Significant, unusual, or highly complex transactions, especially those close to period end that pose difficult "substance over form" questions
  - Significant operations located or conducted across international borders in jurisdictions where differing business environments and cultures exist
  - Significant bank accounts or subsidiary or branch operations in tax-haven jurisdictions for which there appears to be no clear business justification

b. There is ineffective monitoring of management as a result of the following:
  - Domination of management by a single person or small group (in a non-owner-managed business) without compensating controls
  - Ineffective oversight over the financial reporting process and internal control by those charged with governance

c. There is a complex or unstable organizational structure, as evidenced by the following:
  - Difficulty in determining the organization or individuals that have controlling interest in the entity
  - Overly complex organizational structure involving unusual legal entities or managerial lines of authority
  - High turnover of senior management, counsel, or board members

d. Internal control components are deficient as a result of the following:
  - Inadequate monitoring of controls, including automated controls and controls over interim financial reporting (where external reporting is required)
  - High turnover rates or employment of ineffective accounting, internal audit, or information technology staff
  - Ineffective accounting and information systems, including situations involving significant deficiencies or material weaknesses in internal control

Attitudes/Rationalizations

a. Ineffective communication, implementation, support, or enforcement of the entity's values or ethical standards by management or the communication of inappropriate values or ethical standards
b. Nonfinancial management's excessive participation in or preoccupation with the selection of accounting principles or the determination of significant estimates
c. Known history of violations of securities laws or other laws and regulations, or claims against the entity, its senior management, or board members alleging fraud or violations of laws and regulations
d. Excessive interest by management in maintaining or increasing the entity's stock price or earnings trend
e. A practice by management of committing to analysts, creditors, and other third parties to achieve aggressive or unrealistic forecasts
f. Management failing to correct known significant deficiencies or material weaknesses in internal control on a timely basis
g. An interest by management in employing inappropriate means to minimize reported earnings for tax-motivated reasons
h. Recurring attempts by management to justify marginal or inappropriate accounting on the basis of materiality
i. The relationship between management and the current or predecessor auditor is strained, as exhibited by the following:
  - Frequent disputes with the current or predecessor auditor on accounting, auditing, or reporting matters

- Unreasonable demands on the auditor, such as unreasonable time constraints regarding the completion of the audit or the issuance of the auditor's report
- Formal or informal restrictions on the auditor that inappropriately limit access to people or information or the ability to communicate effectively with those charged with governance
- Domineering management behavior in dealing with the auditor, especially involving attempts to influence the scope of the auditor's work or the selection or continuance of personnel assigned to or consulted on the audit engagement

Risk factors relating to misstatements arising from misappropriation of assets

Risk factors that relate to misstatements arising from misappropriation of assets are also classified according to the three conditions generally present when fraud exists: incentives/pressures, opportunities, and attitudes/rationalizations. Some of the risk factors related to misstatements arising from fraudulent financial reporting also may be present when misstatements arising from misappropriation of assets occur. For example, ineffective monitoring of management and weaknesses in internal control may be present when misstatements due to either fraudulent financial reporting or misappropriation of assets exist. The following are examples of risk factors related to misstatements arising from misappropriation of assets.

Incentives/pressures

a. Personal financial obligations may create pressure on management or employees with access to cash or other assets susceptible to theft to misappropriate those assets.
b. Adverse relationships between the entity and employees with access to cash or other assets susceptible to theft may motivate those employees to misappropriate those assets. For example, adverse relationships may be created by the following:
- Known or anticipated future employee layoffs
- Recent or anticipated changes to employee compensation or benefit plans
- Promotions, compensation, or other rewards inconsistent with expectations

Opportunities

a. Certain characteristics or circumstances may increase the susceptibility of assets to misappropriation. For example, opportunities to misappropriate assets increase when there are the following:
- Large amounts of cash on hand or processed
- Inventory items that are small in size, of high value, or in high demand
- Easily convertible assets, such as bearer bonds, diamonds, or computer chips
- Fixed assets that are small in size, marketable, or lacking observable identification of ownership

b. Inadequate internal control over assets may increase the susceptibility of misappropriation of those assets. For example, misappropriation of assets may occur because there is the following:
- Inadequate segregation of duties or independent checks
- Inadequate management oversight of employees responsible for assets, for example, inadequate supervision or monitoring of remote locations
- Inadequate job applicant screening of employees with access to assets
- Inadequate recordkeeping with respect to assets
- Inadequate system of authorization and approval of transactions (for example, in purchasing)
- Inadequate physical safeguards over cash, investments, inventory, or fixed assets
- Lack of complete and timely reconciliations of assets
- Lack of timely and appropriate documentation of transactions, for example, credits for merchandise returns
- Lack of mandatory vacations for employees performing key control functions
- Inadequate management understanding of information technology, which enables information technology employees to perpetrate a misappropriation
- Inadequate access controls over automated records, including controls over and review of computer systems event logs

Attitudes/rationalizations

a. Disregard for the need for monitoring or reducing risks related to misappropriations of assets
b. Disregard for internal control over misappropriation of assets by overriding existing controls or by failing to correct known internal control deficiencies
c. Behavior indicating displeasure or dissatisfaction with the company or its treatment of the employee
d. Changes in behavior or lifestyle that may indicate assets have been misappropriated

Recommended Reading

We provide recommended resources in three categories:

1. Resources most suitable for busy executives, directors, and audit committee members
2. Fraud and corruption risk resources
3. Fraud and corruption control resources

We encourage executives, directors, and audit committee members to consider the resources in all three sections, but those in the first may be most relevant and most useful in the time available.

Resources most suitable for busy executives, directors, and audit committee members

American Institute of Certified Public Accountants (AICPA), *Management Override of Internal Controls: The Achilles' Heel of Fraud Prevention,* 2005, www.aicpa.org/audcommctr/download/achilles_heel.pdf.

Deloitte Financial Advisory Services LLP, *Managing the Business Risk of Fraud: New Guidance for a New Risk Environment,* 2008, www.deloitte.com/dtt/article/0,1002,sid%253D2007%2526cid%253D217964,00.html.

Deloitte Financial Advisory Services LLP, *Financial Fraud: Does an Economic Downturn Mean an Uptick?,* 2008, www.deloitte.com/dtt/article/0,1002,sid%253D2007%2526cid%253D238194,00.html.

Deloitte Forensic Center, *Ten Things About Financial Statement Fraud—Second Edition: A Review of SEC Enforcement Releases,* 2008, www.deloitte.com/us/forensiccenter.

Deloitte Forensic Center, *Ten Things About Fraud Control: How Executives View the "Fraud Control Gap,"* 2007, http://www.deloitte.com/dtt/newsletter/0,1012,sid%253D140674%2526cid%253D190486,00.html.

Deloitte Touche Tohmatsu, *The Risk Intelligent Board: Viewing the World Through Risk-Colored Glasses,* 2008, http://www.deloitte.com/dtt/article/0,1002,cid%253D222456,00,html.

International Chamber of Commerce (ICC)/Transparency International (TI)/The United National Global Compact/World Economic Forum Partnering Against

Corruption Initiative (PACI), *Clean Business Is Good Business: The Business Case Against Corruption,* 2008, www.iccwbo.org/policy/anticorruption/iccccgdi/index.html.

The Institute of Internal Auditors (IIA)/AICPA/Association of Certified Fraud Examiners (ACFE), *Managing the Business Risk of Fraud: A Practical Guide—Executive Summary,* 2008, http://www.theiia.org/guidance/standards-and-guidance/additional-resources/managing-the-business-risk-of-fraud/?search=managing%20fraud%20risk.

Transparency International, "TI Corruption Perceptions Index," 2008, www.transparency.org/policy_research/surveys_indices/cpi.

U.S. Department of Justice, "Corporate Charging Guidelines," 2008, www.usdoj.gov/opa/documents/corp-charging-guidelines.pdf.

U.S. Securities and Exchange Commission, *Commission Guidance Regarding Management's Report on Internal Control Over Financial Reporting Under Section 13(a) or 15(d) of the Securities Exchange Act of 1934* (Release Nos. 33–8810, 34–55929, FR-77; File No. S7–24–06; June 20, 2007), www.sec.gov/rules/interp/2007/33–8810fr.pdf.

Fraud and corruption risk resources

ACFE, *2008 ACFE Report to the Nation on Occupational Fraud & Abuse,* 2008, http://www.acfe.com/rttn/2008-rttn.asp.

Deloitte Forensic Center, *Ten Things About Financial Statement Fraud—Second Edition: A Review of SEC Enforcement Releases,* 2008, http://www.deloitte.com/dtt/article/0,1002,cid%253D182092,00.html.

Deloitte Forensic Center, *Ten Things About Bankruptcy and Fraud: A Review of Bankruptcy Filings,* 2008, http://www.deloitte.com/dtt/article/0,1002,cid%253D182092,00.html.

Deloitte Financial Advisory Services LLP, *Fraud Risk Management in Life Sciences Companies,* 2008, www.deloitte.com/dtt/whitepaper/0,1017,sid%253D2007%2526cid%253D168301,00.html.

Transparency International (TI), "TI Corruption Perceptions Index," 2008, www.transparency.org/policy_research/surveys_indices/cpi.

TI, *Global Corruption Report 2008,* 2008, www.transparency.org/publications/gcr.

Tillman, Robert and Michael Inderguard, *Control Overrides in Financial Statement Fraud, A Report to the Institute for Fraud Prevention,* 2007, St. John's University, www.theifp.org/research%20grants/recentStudies.html.

Wells, Joseph T., *Corporate Fraud Handbook,* 2nd edition, Wiley, 2007.

Fraud and corruption control resources

American Conference Institute, *Conducting Forensic Investigations: Detecting, Responding to and Preventing Financial Fraud,* 2007, www.deloitte.com/dtt/whitepaper/0,1017,sid%253D2007%2526cid%253D153032,00.html.

ACFE/AICPA, *Tone at the Top: How Management Can Prevent Fraud in the Workplace,* 2006, www.acfe.com/fraud/tools.asp (white paper and video).

Committee of Sponsoring Organizations of the Treadway Commission (COSO), *Report of the National Commission on Fraudulent Financial Reporting (Treadway Report)*, 1987, www.coso.org.

COSO, *Internal Control—Integrated Framework*, 1992, www.coso.org.

Deloitte Forensic Center, *Ten Things About Fraud Control: How Executives View the "Fraud Control Gap,"* 2007, http://www.deloitte.com/dtt/article/0,1002,cid% 253D182092,00.html.

Dyck, I.J. Alexander, Adair Morse, and Luigi Zingales, "Who Blows the Whistle on Corporate Fraud?", CRSP Working Paper No. 618, January 2007, http://ssrn. com/abstract=959410.

ICC, *ICC Rules of Conduct and Recommendations for Combating Extortion and Bribery (2005 Edition)*, 2005, www.iccwbo.org/uploadedFiles/ICC/policy/anticorruption/Statements/revised%20ICC%20Rules.pdf.

ICC, *Fighting Corruption: International Corporate Integrity Handbook*, 2008, http://www.iccbooks.com/Product/ProductInfo.aspx?id=533

ICC, *ICC Guidelines on Whistleblowing*, 2008, http://www.iccwbo.org/policy/anticorruption/iccccfee/index.html.

International Federation of Accountants, *Defining and Developing an Effective Code of Conduct for Organizations*, June 2007, www.ifac.org/Store/Details.tmpl? SID=1181654891629338&Cart=11402255363322472.

Law Journal Newsletters—Business Crimes Bulletin, *Fraud Control Gap: Implications for Compliance and Ethics Programs*, 2008, www.deloitte.com/dtt/article/ 0,1002,sid%253D148424%2526cid%253D196255,00.html.

Open Compliance and Ethics Group (OCEG), *Foundation Guidelines Red Book*, version 1.0, 2005, www.oceg.org.

OCEG, *Red Book*, version 2.0 (public exposure draft), 2008, www.oceg.org.

OCEG, *Helpline/Hotline Handbook: Designing, Managing, and Measuring Inquiry and Issue Management Capabilities*, version 1.0, 2007, www.oceg.org.

OCEG, *Internal Audit Guide: Assessing Governance, Risk, Compliance and Ethics Capabilities*, version 1.0, 2007, www.oceg.org.

OCEG, *Measurement & Metrics Guide: Performance Measurement Approach and Metrics for an Integrated Governance, Risk, Compliance and Ethics Capability*, version 1.0, 2007, www.oceg.org.

Security Executive Council, *2007 Corporate Governance and Compliance Hotline Benchmarking Report*, 2007, www.securityexecutivecouncil.com/surveys/hotline07/ hotline07.html.

Standards Australia, *AS 8001–2008 Fraud Corruption and Control*, 2008, www. saiglobal.com/shop/Script/Details.asp?DocN=AS0733785220AT.

The Institute of Internal Auditors (IIA)/AICPA/ACFE, *Managing the Business Risk of Fraud: A Practical Guide*, 2008, http://www.theiia.org/guidance/standards-and-guidance/additional-resources/managing-the-business-risk-of-fraud/ ?search=managing%20fraud%20risk.

The IIA, *International Professional Practices Framework, Practice Advisory 1210.A2–1: Auditor's Responsibilities Relating to Fraud Risk Assessment, Prevention, and Detection*, 2009, www.theiia.org/bookstore/product/international-professional-practices-framework-ippf-1368.cfm.

The IIA, *International Professional Practices Framework, Practice Advisory 1210.A2–2: Auditor's Responsibilities Relating to Fraud Investigation, Reporting, Resolution, and Communication*, 2009, www.theiia.org/bookstore/product/international-professional-practices-framework-ippf-1368.cfm.

The Network, Inc., *Best Practices in Ethics Hotlines*, 2008, www.tnwinc.com/downloads/BestPractices_EthicsHotlines.pdf.

United Nations, *United Nations Convention Against Corruption*, 2003, www.unodc.org/unodc/en/treaties/CAC/index.html.

U.S. Sentencing Commission, *2007 Federal Sentencing Guidelines Manual*, Chapter Eight: Sentencing of Organizations, 2007, www.ussc.gov/orgguide.htm.

World Economic Forum, *Partnering Against Corruption—Principles for Countering Bribery*, 2005, www.weforum.org/en/initiatives/paci/index.htm.

References

Preface

As used in this document, "Deloitte" means Deloitte Financial Advisory Services LLP, a subsidiary of Deloitte LLP. Please see www.deloitte.com/us/about for a detailed description of the legal structure of Deloitte LLP and its subsidiaries.

The *Wall Street Journal* article, "U.S., Other Nations Step Up Bribery Battle," is available at http://www.wsj.com/.

The *Financial Times* article, "Guilty Plea to Bribery Sets Legal Landmark," is available at http://www.ft.com/.

The *CFO* article "Count 'Em: 63 CFOs Convicted in Past 5 Years," is available at http://www.cfo.com/.

Chapter 2: The Growing Risk of Fraud and Corruption

The four trends mentioned in this section—Globalization, Economic Downturns, Risk Management Surprises, & Room for Improvement—were drawn from the Deloitte Financial Advisory Services LLP point of view paper, *Managing the Business Risk of Fraud: New Guidance for a New Risk Environment*, published in 2008, to which the authors of this book contributed. The paper addresses how companies manage their fraud risks, as well as current trends for executives to consider in mitigating these risks.

This point of view paper is available at: http://www.deloitte.com/dtt/article/0,1002,sid%253D2007%2526cid%253D217964,00.html/.

The point of view paper discussed the fraud guidance document, *Managing the Business Risk of Fraud: A Practical Guide,* published in July 2008 by the Institute of Internal Auditors, the American Institute of Certified Public Accountants, and the Association of Certified Fraud Examiners. The guide is available at: http://www.theiia.org/guidance/standards-and-guidance/additional-resources/managing-the-business-risk-of-fraud/?search=managing%20fraud%20risk.

The Department of Justice (DOJ) is a government organization created to ensure the general public of safety from all domestic and foreign threats to security and make certain justice is impartially administered to all Americans. For more information on the DOJ, please visit their website at: http://www.usdoj.gov/.

The publication, *Ten Things about Fraud Control: How Executives View the "Fraud Control Gap"*—authored by the Deloitte Forensic Center in 2007—is a report of a survey of 277 senior executives involved in fraud control. The compilation of data used for the report was summarized to identify leading practices in a variety of aspects of fraud control. The report can be downloaded at: http://www.deloitte.com/dtt/article/0,1002,cid%253D182092,00.html.

The Deloitte Forensic Center is a think tank aimed at exploring new approaches for mitigating the costs, risks, and effects of fraud, corruption, and other issues facing the global business community. The Center aims to advance the state of thinking in areas such as fraud and corruption by exploring issues from the perspective of forensic accountants, corporate leaders, and other professionals involved in forensic matters. The Deloitte Forensic Center is sponsored by Deloitte Financial Advisory Services LLP.

Standard and Poor's provides investment research and credit ratings for companies throughout the world. They are also world-renowned for their fixed income, alternative, and equity indices to measure market performance—including the S&P 500. Their website is located at: http://www.standardandpoors.com/.

The fraud schemes and related definitions are taken from a Deloitte and Touche LLP white paper, *Antifraud Programs & Controls,* published in 2004. The white paper is intended for internal auditors and company management looking for specific examples and considerations to take note of when developing anti-fraud programs and controls.

Chapter 3: The Costs of Fraud and Corruption

Statistics and the "Distribution of Dollar Loss" chart displayed in this subchapter are drawn from the *2008 Report to the Nation on Occupational Fraud & Abuse*, authored by the Association of Certified Fraud Examiners (ACFE).

This report, the latest in a series of reports issued by the ACFE every two years, researches the monetary cost of occupational fraud and how fraud is committed. Other sections detail the detection of fraud schemes and profile types of organizations that are frequently victimized by fraud. The report can be found on the ACFE website at: http://www. acfe.com/rttn/2008-rttn.asp.

As mentioned in the subchapter Accounting and Auditing Enforcement Releases (AAERs) are issued when a company has been found guilty of committing an accounting-related crime. All AAERs are located under the SEC website at: http://www.sec.gov/.

As mentioned in the report, the Enron scandal not only forced Enron to cease operations, the accounting firm Arthur Andersen LLP lost its business as well. The financial effects of the Enron scandal are massive—stockholders lost $60 billion in shareholder value while employees lost $2 billion in pension benefits. Arthur Andersen relinquished its licenses to practice as a Certified Public Accounting firm in the United States. The scandal was the main catalyst in the passing of the Sarbanes-Oxley Act of 2002.

The information of executive officer convictions was sourced from an online report from Kate Plourd, *Count Em: 63 CFOs Convicted in Past Five Years*, CFO.com, August 3, 2007.

The *National Law Journal* is a publication directed toward providing relevant legal news of national importance to attorneys. Their website is located at: http://www.nlj.com/.

The data in the chart appearing in this section is pulled from the *Report to the President—Corporate Fraud Task Force 2008*. The report summarizes fraud enforcement actions brought against particular firms and individuals since July 2002.

The Corporate Fraud Task Force, created under President Bush as a subordinate of the Department of Justice, was formed on July 9, 2002, "to strengthen the efforts of the Department of Justice and Federal, State, and local agencies to investigate and prosecute significant financial crimes, recover the proceeds of such crimes, and ensure just and effective punishment of those who perpetrate financial crimes." The full-length version of the report can be found on the Department of Justice's website at: http://www.usdoj.gov/.

Chapter 4: Building a Resilient Corporation

Various parts of this chapter were drawn from the Deloitte Financial Advisory Services LLP point of view paper, *Managing the Business Risk of Fraud: New Guidance for a New Risk Environment*, published in 2008, to which the authors of this book contributed. The paper addresses how companies manage their fraud risks, as well as current trends for executives to consider in mitigating these risks.

This point of view paper is also referenced in the "Five Principles of Fraud Risk Management," "The First Line of Defense," "How Can Companies Use the New Guidance?" and "Building Resiliency by Enhancing Fraud and Corruption Risk Management sections". The Real-World Example insets and the Measure Improve and Move Methodology table also source the paper.

The five principles of fraud risk management were reproduced from the fraud guidance document, *Managing the Business Risk of Fraud: A Practical Guide*, published in July 2008 by the Institute of Internal Auditors, the American Institute of Certified Public Accountants, and the Association of Certified Fraud Examiners. The guide is available at: http://www.theiia.org/guidance/standards-and-guidance/additional-resources/managing-the-business-risk-of-fraud/?search=managing%20fraud%20risk.

Section 301 of the Sarbanes-Oxley Act of 2002 establishes standards relating to audit committees including independence standards, establishing whistle-blower hotlines, and the authority to engage legal counsel. A downloadable PDF version of the act is available at: http://www.pcaobus.org/.

The SEC has issued guidance increasing the responsibilities of audit committees. An example of one such pronouncement is Final Rule 33-8817: Disclosures Required by Sections 406 and 407 of the Sarbanes-Oxley Act of 2002. In this rule, audit committees must disclose whether a financial expert currently serves on the audit committee. For more information on audit committee responsibilities, visit the SEC Final Rules website at: http://www.sec.gov/rules/final.shtml/.

Both the NYSE and NASDAQ exchanges require the audit committees of their listed companies to adhere to strict guidelines. Listing information for both exchanges is available at their respective websites:
- NYSE: http://www.nyse.com/
- NASDAQ: http://www.nasdaq.com/

Chapter 5: Fraud and Corruption Risk Assessment

The Committee of Sponsoring Organizations of the Treadway Commission, or COSO, is a voluntary private-sector organization that provides in-depth analysis and research on corporate governance best practices to improve organizational operations. For more information on COSO, please visit their website at: http://www.coso.org/.

As mentioned in the book, these Code of Ethics definitions were pulled from the SEC Final Rule 33-8810: Commission Guidance Regarding Management's Report on Internal Control Over Financial Reporting Under Section 13(a) or 15(d) of the Securities Exchange Act of 1934. The rule establishes a framework for companies to organize a top-down, risk-based approach evaluation of internal control over financial reporting. The interpretative guideline in the final rule complies with the requirements set forth by Rules 13a-15(c) and 15d-15(c) under the Securities Exchange Act of 1934.

All SEC final rules are located under the SEC website at: http://www.sec.gov/rules/final.shtml/.

For our discussion of the fraud and corruption risk assessment overview, we relied heavily on our personal knowledge of the matter. We also found other sources useful such as U.S. Auditing Standards AU316, *Consideration of Fraud in a Financial Statement Audit,* and *Managing the Business Risk of Fraud: A Practical Guide,* published in July 2008 by the Institute of Internal Auditors, the American Institute of Certified Public Accountants, and the Association of Certified Fraud Examiners. The guide is available at http://www.theiia.org/guidance/standards-and-guidance/additional-resources/managing-the-business-risk-of-fraud/?search=managing%20fraud%20risk.

The authors were referring to a 1999 study performed by professors Mark S. Beasley, Joseph V. Carcello, and Dana R. Hermanson and sponsored by the Committee of Sponsoring Organizations of the Treadway Commission (COSO), titled *Fraudulent Financial Reporting 1987–1997: An Analysis of U.S. Public Companies.* The objectives of the report were to identify key company/management characteristics of the companies involved in instances of financial statement fraud and provide an opinion to improve financial reporting based on all findings. A PDF version of the report is available at: http://www.coso.org/publications/FFR_1987_1997.PDF.

A follow-up study covering the subsequent period is scheduled for publication in the first quarter of 2009 and is expected to be available at http://www.coso.org/.

The Sarbanes-Oxley Act of 2002 (SOX) was passed into federal law in the wake of devastating accounting scandals such as Enron, Tyco International, Adelphia, and WorldCom. Some of the main tenets of the law include auditor independence, corporate responsibility, internal control, and the creation of the Public Company Accounting Oversight Board (PCAOB). A downloadable PDF version is available at: http://www.pcaobus.org/.

SEC Final Rules are those rules that the governing body has agreed upon. For a listing of all rules, please visit: http://www.sec.gov/rules/final.shtml/.

SAS 99, *Consideration of Fraud in a Financial Statement Audit,* sets out procedures for external auditors to follow when conducting financial statement audits. SAS 99 has been codified into Statements on Auditing Standards, Section AU316. For more information, please visit: http://www.aicpa.org/.

PCAOB Auditing Standard No. 5, *An Audit of Internal Control Over Financial Reporting That Is Integrated with an Audit of Financial Statements,* was approved by the Securities and Exchange Commission in July 2007. The pronouncement aims to guide auditors by setting out requirements and items that should be considered when planning and executing an audit of management's assessment of internal controls over financial reporting. PCAOB Auditing Standard No. 5 is available at the PCAOB website at: http://www.pcaobus.org/.

The Committee of Sponsoring Organizations of the Treadway Commission (COSO) is a voluntary private-sector organization that provides in-depth analysis and research on corporate governance best practices to improve organizational operations. For more information on COSO, please visit their website at: http://www.coso.org/.

Chapter 6: Company-wide Anti-Fraud Controls: The Role of the Control Environment and High-Level Strategies

For this discussion of the qualities of a strong control environment, we relied on a Deloitte & Touche LLP white paper, *Antifraud Programs & Controls.* The white paper, published in 2004, is intended for internal auditors and company management looking for specific examples and considerations to take note of when developing anti-fraud programs and controls.

This white paper is also cited in other sections within this chapter, including "Tone at the Top," "The Control Environment and Governance," and "Setting the Tone."

PCAOB Auditing Standard No. 5, *An Audit of Internal Control Over Financial Reporting That Is Integrated with an Audit of Financial Statements,* was approved by the Securities and Exchange Commission in July 2007. The pronouncement aims to guide auditors by setting out requirements and items that should be considered when planning and executing an audit of management's assessment of internal controls over financial reporting. PCAOB Auditing Standard No. 5 is available at the PCAOB website at: http://www.pcaobus.org/.

The material in this subchapter was drawn from the fraud guidance paper, *Managing the Business Risk of Fraud: A Practical Guide*, published in July 2008 by the Institute of Internal Auditors, the American Institute of Certified Public Accountants, and the Association of Certified Fraud Examiners. The guide is available at: http://www.theiia.org/ guidance/standards-and-guidance/additional-resources/managing-the-business-risk-of-fraud/?search=managing% 20fraud%20risk.

This section on fraud risk governance indicates the objectives that should be met from an effective fraud risk management program. Within the discussion is an analysis of the roles that the board of directors, audit committee, management, staff, and internal auditors all play in supporting the program.

Sections 406 and 407 of the Sarbanes-Oxley Act of 2002 relate to a code of ethics for senior financial officers and disclosure of an audit committee financial expert, respectively. For more information about these sections and the pronouncement, please visit: http://www.pcaobus.org/.

Parts of this discussion were drawn from *Developing a Fraud Risk Management Program for Your Organization*, a fraud education seminar developed on behalf of Deloitte & Touche LLP by Deloitte Financial Advisory Services LLP for the Institute of Internal Auditors. The authors of this book contributed to the development of this seminar.

This source has also been referenced in the subchapters "Fundamentals of GRC," and "Integrated versus Nonintegrated GRC."

As mentioned in the book, these Code of Ethics definitions were pulled from the SEC Final Rule 31-8177: Disclosure Required by Sections 406 and 407 of the Sarbanes-Oxley Act of 2002. The rule mandates all SEC registrants, other than registered investment companies, to include two types of disclosures in their annual financial statements. The first required disclosure is if an audit committee has at least one financial expert serving on the committee and whether he or she is independent of management. The second disclosure will indicate whether a company has adopted a code of ethics.

All SEC final rules are located under the SEC website at: http://www.sec.gov/rules/final.shtml/.

As mentioned in the book, Section 301 of the Sarbanes-Oxley Act of 2002 requires audit committees to establish procedures for anonymous complaints. The pronouncement in its entirety can be located at: http://www.pcaobus.org/.

The U. S. Sentencing Commission is an independent organization serving under the judicial branch of government. One of their main responsibilities is setting sentencing standards for violators of federal crimes. For more information, please visit their website at: http://www.ussc.gov/.

Established in 1941, the Institute of Internal Auditors (IIA) is an international professional association of more than 150,000 members with global headquarters in Florida in the United States. Throughout the world, the IIA is recognized as the internal audit profession's leader in certification, education, research, and technical guidance. For more information, please visit their website at: http://www.theiia.org/.

For this section, we relied on *Enterprise Risk Management— Integrated Framework: Executive Summary*, a study authored in 2004 by PricewaterhouseCoopers (PwC) for the Committee of Sponsoring Organizations of the Treadway Commission (COSO) to provide companies with an overview of risk management for various enterprises.

The paper primarily focuses on defining risk management practices for enterprises and analyzing how the specific objectives and components of enterprise risk management (ERM) are interrelated.

The electronic version of the article is available at the following website: http://www.coso.org/.

The goals of an Enterprise Risk Management (ERM) program were drawn from the Deloitte & Touche LLP white paper, *Assessing the Value of Enterprise Risk Management.* The paper, written in 2004 in cooperation with the Economist Intelligence Unit (EIU), analyzes the benefits and costs of implementing ERM within their fraud risk assessments. The paper also introduces real-world case scenarios of companies that have benefited from implementing ERM.

The designation *risk intelligence enterprises* and its characteristics were pulled from *The Risk Intelligent Enterprise—ERM Done Right,* a Deloitte & Touche LLP 2006 study highlighting the leading practices of firms that effectively implement ERM to regularly assess and manage their fraud risks.

Also included in the study are points to define risk, avoid silos, and establish fundamental steps to improve ERM within a company.

The authors reference viewing Government, Risk, and Compliance (GRC) "as a system of related functions, with common activities, best approached in a comprehensive, holistic manner." The authors are directly referring to a Deloitte-sponsored illustration, entitled *Making the Business Case for Integrated GRC,* emphasizing the drivers necessary in order to streamline and integrate processes, lower costs, and enhance greater transparency and visibility of business operations.

The illustration is available at: http://www.deloitte.com/.

Deloitte LLP published in 2008 a book directed at top executives looking to bolster their corporate governance, risk, and compliance procedures. *Growing Confidence: The Smart Way to Manage Governance, Risk and Compliance* helps executives understand emerging business trends and issues that could potentially develop into unforeseen risks. The book offers advice for boards to consider in their efforts to improve GRC processes against silos and the lack of information necessary to identify fraud risks.

The book *Growing Confidence: The Smart Way to Manage Governance, Risk and Compliance* is available as a PDF download at: http://www.deloitte.com/straighttalk/.

The survey referenced in the text is a 2007 OCEG GRC Strategy Study conducted by the Open Compliance and Ethics Group (OCEG), sponsored by Deloitte LLP, SAP, and Cisco. The survey questioned 250 professionals with the objective of creating benchmarks of companies' governance, risk, and compliance (GRC) processes to compare with global organizations and other peers.

A free copy (registration required) of the report is available at: http:www.oceg.org/Details/20056.

OCEG is a nonprofit organization offering guidance, standards, benchmarks, and tools for integrating governance, risk management, internal control, and compliance (GRC) processes. For more information about the organization, please visit: http://www.oceg.org/.

Various parts in this section were referenced from the World Economic Forum Partnering Against Corruption Initiative (PACI) website. For more information about PACI, please visit: http://www.weforum.org/en/initiatives/paci/index.htm/.

The Ferdinando Nani Becalli interview was provided in the Nigerian politically based publication, *This Day*, and can be found at: http://www.thisdayonline.com/.

Chapter 7: Preventive Controls: Particular Fraud and Corruption Avoidance Strategies and Tactics

As mentioned in the chapter, the trader who made an unauthorized trade on wheat futures reportedly lost MF Global $141.5 million. For a more in-depth discussion of this article, please visit: http://www.chicagotribune.com/.

For our discussion on preventive controls, we turned to *Managing the Business Risk of Fraud: A Practical Guide*, published in July 2008 by the Institute of Internal Auditors, the American Institute of Certified Public Accountants, and the Association of Certified Fraud Examiners. The guide is available at: http://www.theiia.org/guidance/standards-and-guidance/additional-resources/managing-the-business-risk-of-fraud/?search=managing%20fraud%20risk.

This report has also been referenced in the subchapter "Confronting Fraud and Corruption Risks."

As mentioned in the chapter, the ACFE's *2008 Report to the Nation on Occupational Fraud & Abuse* goes into great depth to demonstrate the monetary cost of occupational fraud and how it is committed. Other sections detail the detection of fraud schemes and the types of organizations that are frequently victimized by fraud. The report can be found on the ACFE website at: http://www.acfe.com/rttn/2008-rttn.asp.

Ethical Business Practice: Importance for the Recruiting Process was produced by the Institute for Ethical Business Worldwide at the University of Notre Dame's Mendoza College of Business, in collaboration with the Ethics Resource Center and the Business Roundtable's Institute for Corporate Ethics. It is available at http://www.ethicalbuisness.nd.edu/pdf/Ethical%20Bus%20Prac.pdf

PCAOB Auditing Standard No. 5, *An Audit of Internal Control Over Financial Reporting That Is Integrated with an Audit of Financial Statements* was approved by the Securities and Exchange Commission in July 2007. The pronouncement aims to guide auditors by setting out requirements and items that should be considered when planning and executing an audit of management's assessment of internal controls over financial reporting. PCAOB Auditing Standard No. 5 is available at the PCAOB website at: http://www.pcaobus.org/.

As mentioned in the chapter, we pulled information from *American Metal Market* magazine relating to three employees selling proprietary trade secrets to a competitor. The article is available online at the American Metals Markets website at: http://www.amm.com/.

COSO Guidance on Monitoring Internal Control Systems was released in 2009 following a 1992 COSO publication, *Internal Control— Integrated Framework*. The purpose of this white paper was to further elaborate the monitoring component of the COSO internal control framework. The objective of the report was twofold: to improve the efficiency and effectiveness of organizational internal control systems and to identify and demonstrate monitoring practices that can be intertwined into internal control processes. A free online executive summary of this report can be accessed at: http://www.coso.org/.

Though largely anecdotal, the table provided in this subchapter is courtesy of *The Risk Intelligent Enterprise—ERM Done Right,* a 2006 Deloitte & Touche LLP publication highlighting the leading practices of firms that effectively implement Enterprise Risk Management (ERM) to regularly assess and manage their risks. The publication is available at: http://www.deloitte.com/dtt/article/ 0,1002,cid%253D119871,00.html.

Chapter 8: Detective Controls and Transaction Monitoring

As directly mentioned in the chapter, statistics in this subchapter are drawn from the *2008 Report to the Nation on Occupational Fraud & Abuse*, authored by the Association of Certified Fraud Examiners (ACFE). For a downloadable PDF version of the report, please refer to the ACFE website at: http://www.acfe.com/rttn/2008-rttn.asp.

Section 301 of the Sarbanes-Oxley Act of 2002 establishes standards relating to audit committees establishing whistle-blower hotlines. A downloadable PDF version of the act is available at: http://www.pcaobus.org/.

The 2007 Deloitte Forensic Center study referred to in the book is *Ten Things About Fraud Control: How Executives View the 'Fraud Control Gap.'* The study surveyed hundreds of executives involved with fraud controls to assess the level of their companies' effectiveness of managing fraud. The Deloitte Forensic Center then developed key findings and observations from the survey. This report is available at: http://www.deloitte.com/dtt/article/0,1002,cid%253D182092,00.html.

The Institute of Internal Auditors' Professional Practice Framework consists of mandatory guidance and strongly recommended guidance. Within the mandatory category is the Code of Ethics and Standards portions. For more information, visit: www.theiia.org/bookstore/product/international-professional-practices-framework-ippf-1368.cfm.

Moore's law refers to the advance in computer processing power per unit cost. Moore's law is based on the statement by Gordon Moore, co-founder of Intel Corporation, who predicted that computer memory will double in computing capacity while halving in cost approximately every 18 months.

For parts of this discussion, we turned to the Deloitte article, *Continuous Fraud Monitoring: A Real-Time Solution to a Real Problem?* published in 2007 in *Consulting* magazine. This article is available at: http://www.theiia.org/chapters/pub-docs/241/CFM.pdf.

Chapter 9: Preparing for Fraud and Corruption Investigations and Remediation

The leading practices in this section were adapted from *Managing the Business Risk of Fraud: A Practical Guide,* published in July 2008 by the Institute of Internal Auditors, the American Institute of Certified Public Accountants, and the Association of Certified Fraud Examiners. The guide is available at: http://www.theiia.org/guidance/standards-and-guidance/additional-resources/managing-the-business-risk-of-fraud/?search=managing%20fraud%20risk.

Deloitte Financial Advisory Services LLP published in 2007 a white paper that dives further into responding to fraud investigations, entitled, *What to Do When Regulators Come Knocking.* A downloadable PDF version of this article is available at: http://www.deloitte.com/dtt/cda/doc/content/us_fas_regulators_white_paper_070207.pdf.

We recommend reading the Deloitte Financial Advisory Services LLP point of view paper *Managing the Business Risk of Fraud: New Guidance for a New Risk Environment* for a more in-depth discussion of the topic. A downloadable PDF version of this article is available at: www.deloitte.com/dtt/article/0,1002,sid%253D2007%2526cid%253D217964,00.html.

Chapter 10: The Players' Roles (Including Yours)

For a transcript of the Harvey Pitt speech, in addition to other SEC speeches and public statements, please visit: http://www.sec.gov/.

For the discussion of NYSE and NASDAQ standards, we relied on *New Corporate Governance Listing Standards—Audit Committee Handbook,* a publication authored in 2004 by Deloitte & Touche LLP. This report summarizes the audit committee responsibilities set forth in the NYSE and

NASDAQ corporate listing standards, in addition to actions to consider when implementing the requirements and resources and tools to use as a reference.

As mentioned in the section, the excerpt was taken from *Managing the Business Risk of Fraud: A Practical Guide*, published in July 2008 by the Institute of Internal Auditors, the American Institute of Certified Public Accountants, and the Association of Certified Fraud Examiners. The guide is available at: http://www.theiia.org/guidance/standards-and-guidance/ additional-resources/managing-the-business-risk-of-fraud/ ?search=managing%20fraud%20risk.

This source is also referenced in the "Fraud and Corruption Risk Management Is Everyone's Business" subchapter.

Section 404 of the Sarbanes-Oxley Act (SOX) of 2002, Management Assessment of Internal Controls, is one of the most important tenets of SOX. The pronouncement, in its entirety, is available at: http://www.pcaobus.org/.

As mentioned in the book, this excerpt was pulled from the SEC Final Rule 33-8238: *Management's Reports on Internal Control Over Financial Reporting and Certification of Disclosure in Exchange Act Periodic Reports.* The report discusses the responsibilities of the external auditor and management when conducting a report of internal control and the disclosures necessary to fulfill all Section 404 requirements.

All SEC final rules are located under the SEC website at: http://www.sec.gov/rules/final.shtml/.

For extra reading on the Oil-for-Food program scandal, please refer to *Good Intentions Corrupted: The Oil-for-Food Scandal and the Threat to the U.N.*, by Jeffrey A. Meyer and Mark G. Califano, with an introduction by Paul A. Volcker, published in the United States (New York, 2006) by PublicAffairs, a member of the Perseus Books Group.

Parts of the section were drawn from PCAOB Auditing Standard No. 5, *An Audit of Internal Control Over Financial Reporting That Is Integrated with an Audit of Financial Statements* which was approved by the Securities and Exchange Commission in July 2007. The pronouncement aims to guide auditors by setting out requirements and items that should be considered when planning and executing an audit of management's assessment of internal controls over financial reporting. PCAOB Auditing Standard No. 5 is available at the PCAOB website at: http://www.pcaobus.org/.

Conclusion—What the Future May Hold

Transparency International (TI) is an organization whose mission is to create change with the hope of eradicating corruption. The scale that the authors were referring to is the Corruption Perceptions Index—an index that employs expert assessments and surveys to rank 180 countries based on their perceived level of corruption. For more information on the scale and TI in general, please visit: http://www .transparency.org/.

Disclosure

This publication contains general information only and Deloitte Financial Advisory Services LLP, its affiliates and related entities are not, by means of this publication, rendering accounting, business, financial, investment, legal, tax, or other professional advice or services. This publication is not a substitute for such professional advice or services, nor should it be used as a basis for any decision or action that may affect your business. Before making any decision or taking any action that may affect your business, you should consult a qualified professional advisor. Deloitte Financial Advisory Services LLP, its affiliates and related entities shall not be responsible for any loss sustained by any person who relies on this publication. The views expressed in this publication are solely those of the authors and not necessarily those of Deloitte Financial Advisory Services LLP, its affiliates and related entities.

About Deloitte

Deloitte refers to one or more of Deloitte Touche Tohmatsu, a Swiss Verein, and its network of member firms, each of which is a legally separate and independent entity. Please see www.deloitte.com/about for a detailed description of the legal structure of Deloitte Touche Tohmatsu and its member firms. Please see www.deloitte.com/us/about for a detailed description of the legal structure of Deloitte LLP and its subsidiaries.

About the Deloitte Forensic Center

The Deloitte Forensic Center is a think tank aimed at exploring new approaches for mitigating the costs, risks, and effects of fraud, corruption, and other issues facing the global business community. The Center aims to advance the state of thinking in areas such as fraud and corruption by exploring issues from the perspective of forensic accountants, corporate leaders, and other professionals involved in forensic matters. The Deloitte Forensic Center is sponsored by Deloitte Financial Advisory Services LLP. Please see www. deloitte.com/forensiccenter for more information.

About the Authors

Toby J.F. Bishop

Toby Bishop is the director of the Deloitte Forensic Center for Deloitte Financial Advisory Services LLP. He is a contributing author and a member of the board of editors of *Business Crimes Bulletin*. He has been named five times to *Accounting Today*'s Top 100 Most Influential People in the Accounting Profession.

Toby is the former president and chief executive officer of the Association of Certified Fraud Examiners (ACFE), the global professional association of nearly 50,000 anti-fraud professionals in 125 countries. He is a global thought leader in the area of fraud prevention and detection and provides education on this topic for executives, boards, and audit committees.

Toby co-authored the American Institute of Certified Public Accountants' (AICPA) guidance, *Management Antifraud Programs and Controls: Guidance to Help Prevent, Deter, and Detect Fraud*, as well as *Management Override: The Achilles' Heel of Fraud Prevention—The Audit Committee and Oversight of Financial Reporting*. He also co-authored the Institute of Internal Auditors/AICPA/ACFE 2008 guidance paper, *Managing the Business Risk of Fraud: A Practical Guide*.

Toby has been quoted in major international publications such as the *New York Times*, London's *Daily Telegraph*, and *India Today*. He has spoken around the world about fraud issues and has appeared on television in several countries.

A native of England, Toby is a graduate of Oxford University. He is a Certified Public Accountant licensed in Illinois and Massachusetts, a Certified Fraud Examiner, and a fellow of the Institute of Chartered Accountants in England & Wales.

Frank E. Hydoski

Frank Hydoski is the national leader of Deloitte Financial Advisory Services LLP's Analytic and Forensic Technology practice group, as well as an advisor to the Deloitte Forensic Center. He is responsible for developing new products and approaches in forensic accounting and investigations for clients in both the private and public sector. Internationally recognized for his work in complex investigations, Frank has guided a number of high-profile investigations.

As chief of forensics for the committee examining the United Nations Oil-for-Food Programme, Frank worked directly under Paul Volcker and was responsible for forensic accounting tasks as well as the development of analytical databases designed to combine all available information about contracts and transactions underlying the program.

Frank also led a crucial part of the massive forensic effort in the investigation of Holocaust-era accounts held by Swiss banks. One of the largest investigations of its kind, Frank's team used forensic techniques to reconstruct the activity of more than 800,000 Holocaust-era accounts at one of the largest banks in Switzerland. Of these, tens of thousands were identified as possibly belonging to victims of Nazi persecution.

Frank was a keynote speaker at the Association of Certified Fraud Examiners' 2006 Annual Conference. He has been prominently featured in *Fraud* magazine, *Business Finance, Consulting* magazine, and *CIO Insights*. His most recent publications include a chapter, with Mary Jane Schirber, on identifying and quantifying assets in *Recovering Stolen Assets*, edited by Mark Pieth, and a chapter, with Yogesh Bahl, on forensic accounting in litigations, investigations, and compliance matters in the new edition of the *Accountant's Handbook*.

Frank is a graduate of San Diego State University and the University of Chicago, with a Ph.D. degree from the latter. He is a member of Phi Beta Kappa and is also an associate member of the ACFE and the AICPA.

Index

A

Accelerated filers, 146
Access controls, 99
Accountability, 16, 42
Accounts affected by fraud, identifying, 54, 55
Ahmed, Mohammed, 17
American Institute of Certified Public Accountants (AICPA)
  Managing the Business Risk of Fraud: A Practical Guide. See Managing the Business Risk of Fraud: A Practical Guide
  Professional Standards, 144
Anti-fraud tactics versus anti-fraud strategies, 5, 6
Arthur Andersen LLP, 26
Assessment. *See* Risk assessment
Asset misappropriation
  and level of fraud, 19
  preventive controls, 98, 99
  risk factors for, 165–167
Association of Certified Fraud Examiners (ACFE)
  2008 Report to the Nation on Occupational Fraud and Abuse, 19, 21, 22, 78, 93, 96, 106, 107
  Managing the Business Risk of Fraud: A Practical Guide. See Managing the Business Risk of Fraud: A Practical Guide

Occupational Fraud and Abuse Classification System, 96, 97
Attitude as risk factor, 50, 164–167
Audit committee
  background investigation of members, 80
  board of directors, relationship with, 154
  code of ethics, responsibility for, 74
  internal audit, oversight of, 70, 110, 143
  investigation oversight, 125, 127
  listing standard requirements, 138
  management override, oversight of controls for preventing, 45, 101
  monitoring activities, oversight of, 121
  notifying of alleged fraud, 124, 125
  and principles of fraud risk management, 38
  and response plan, 124, 125
  responsibilities of, 70, 138, 139
  role of in fraud investigations, 125, 127, 128
  role of in risk assessment, 52–54
  role of in risk management, 39, 41, 52, 53, 68, 69, 136, 138, 139, 148

Audit committee (*continued*)
tone at the top, setting, 71, 139.
See also Tone at the top
whistle-blower hotline,
responsibility for, 78,
108–110
Auditing Standard AS No. 5, 145
Auditing Standard AU 110, 145
Auditing Standard AU 316,
*Consideration of Fraud in a
Financial Statement Audit*, 51,
55, 145
*Australian Standard 8001-2008 Fraud
and Corruption Control*, 71
Automation
detective controls, 112
effectiveness of automated
controls, 80
electronic information,
collection of for
investigations, 124
GRC (governance, risk and
compliance) monitoring, 88
monitoring activities, 102
preventive controls, 96
transaction monitoring, 115
Avoiding problems, 33
Awareness
of effective detective controls as
deterrent, 10, 39, 92
fraud awareness training, 15, 40,
41, 71, 77, 95
importance of, 16–18

B

Background checks
board of directors, members
of, 80
and due diligence, 95
employees, 80, 95
partners, agents, and vendors, 99

Bankruptcy as a consequence of
financial statement fraud,
23, 115
Basel Institute on Governance, 88
Beccalli, Ferdinando Nani, 88
Biegelman, Martin, 26, 37
Boak, Joshua, 92
Board of directors
audit committee, relationship
with, 154
background investigation of
members of, 80
investigation oversight, 127
and response plan,
124, 125
role of in fraud investigation,
123–125, 127, 128
role of in risk assessment, 139
role of in risk management, 38,
39, 41, 138–140
and stock exchange listing
standards, 138
Brasseur, Olivier, 18, 68
Bribery and corruption. *See also*
Foreign Corrupt Practices Act
(FCPA)
and corporate-level self-imposed
anti-fraud programs,
88, 89
data interrogation techniques
for detecting, 116, 117
fines and penalties, 26, 27
and fraud, 5
global trends, xv
Mexico, 48
and multinational companies, 15
penalties for, 7
preventive controls, 99, 100
treaties and legislation, 16
Budget constraints, 144
Buffett, Warren, 68

C

Capital, cost and availability of, 25
Case management systems, 124, 133, 134
Cash, preventive controls for, 99
Chief executive officer (CEO)
  certification of financial statements, 140
  and tone at the top, 141. *See also* Tone at the top
Chief financial officer (CFO)
  background investigation of, 80
  certification of financial statements, 140
Class-action litigation, 23
Classification of fraud and abuse, 96, 97
Code of ethics. *See also* Ethics
  contents of, 75
  creating, 76, 77
  defined, 74
  Deloitte Code of Ethics and Professional Conduct, 75, 76
  as deterrent to wrongdoing, 74
  and employee discipline, 81
  enforcement of, responsibility for, 141
  importance of, 74, 75
  purpose of, 74
Coleman, Bill, 113
Collusion, 94, 114, 115, 145, 148
Committee of Sponsoring Organizations of the Treadway Commission (COSO), 46, 54, 69. *See also* COSO framework
Commodity Futures Trading Commission, fraud investigations, 27
Common sense, 17, 18
Communications, investigation team, 133

Competitive advantage, xxiv, 152
Compliance officer, role of, 147, 148
Computer forensics, 124, 130, 131
Condon, Kevin, 130, 131, 133
Consultants, use of, 146, 154
Continuous auditing, 112
Continuous controls monitoring (CCM)
  continuous fraud monitoring distinguished, 118
  and data quality, 113, 114
  described, 102, 103
Continuous fraud monitoring (CFM)
  advantages of, 119
  and artificial intelligence technologies, 118
  candidates for, 119, 120
  continuous controls monitoring distinguished, 118
  described, 117, 118
  discrete fraud detection compared, 118
  lookbacks as control check, 120, 121
  rules-based, 119
Continuous improvement approach (Measure, Improve, and Move methodology), 40, 41
Continuous monitoring, 112
Control environment
  as a bulwark, 69, 70
  described, 67, 68
  and effectiveness of risk management program, 69, 70
  employee selection and discipline, 80, 81
  and enterprise risk management (ERM), 82–84
  as fraud deterrent, 67, 70, 88
  and fraud risk factors, 52
  and governance, 70

Control environment (*continued*)
  governance, risk and
    compliance (GRC) approach,
    84–88
  hotlines, 78, 79. *See also* Whistle-
    blower hotlines (helplines)
  human resources, role of,
    80, 81
  importance of, 67, 157
  and Partnering Against
    Corruption Initiative (PACI),
    88, 89
  purpose of controls, 93
  risk management program, 71
  and tone at the top, 68, 69,
    71–74. *See also* Tone at the top
  training, 77
  whistle-blower protection, 79
  written policies, 71
Controllers, background
  investigation of, 80
Cooking the books, 52, 54, 57, 63
Core competency, fraud risk
  management as, 17
Corporate agility, need for, 7
Corporate culture
  cultural preparedness, 160
  ethics, 35, 68
  and tone at the top, 68, 69,
    71–74. *See also* Tone at the top
Corporate Fraud Task Force, 26
Corporate governance. *See*
  Governance
Corruption. *See* Bribery and
  corruption
COSO framework
  control environment as key
    component of, 69
  *Guidance on Monitoring Internal
    Control Systems*, 101, 103
  monitoring anti-fraud programs
    and controls, 100, 101

risk assessment as part of
  anti-fraud program, 46
Costs of fraud and corruption
  and benefits of risk
    management, 35
  capital, cost and availability of, 25
  criminal liability, 26–28
  future cost, 22–23
  generally, xxi, xxii, 6
  personal costs, 26–28
  and public opinion, 26
  statistics, 20–22
Criminal liability
  bribery and corruption, 7, 26, 27
  corporate liability, 26, 27
  corporate officers and legal
    counsel, 26
  fines and penalties, 26–28
  incarceration rates, 27
  personal costs, 28
  trend toward aggressive
    enforcement, 27
Crisis management, 125
C-SOX, compliance with and
  benefits of risk management,
  35
Cultural differences
  double accounting systems, 54
  and globalization, 5

D

Dashboards, use of, 42
Data analytics, 112, 113
Data integrity, 113
Data interrogation
  FCPA and other corruption
    violations, 116, 117
  financial statement fraud,
    115, 116
  money laundering, 116
  procurement fraud, 114, 115
  techniques generally, 113, 114

Data mining, 112, 113
Delisting, 23
Deloitte Code of Ethics and Professional Conduct, 75, 76
Deloitte Forensic Center (DFC)
 studies on financial statement fraud, 23, 24, 32, 107
 Ten Things About Fraud Control (2007 survey), 14, 35
 web site, 156
Dent, Peter, 153
Department of Energy, fraud investigations, 27
Department of Justice
 corporate fraud convictions, 26
 fraud investigations, 27
Department of Labor, fraud investigations, 27
Department of the Treasury, fraud investigations, 27
Detection of fraud
 common areas for improvement, 40
 controls. *See* Detective controls
 and duration of fraud, statistics on, 107
 as element of fraud and corruption risk management, 10
 principles of risk management, 37, 38
 tools for, 63
 whistle-blower hotlines. *See* Whistle-blower hotlines (helplines)
Detective controls
 automated transaction monitoring, 115
 continuous fraud monitoring, 117–121
 data interrogation techniques, 113–117

 as deterrent to fraud, 10, 39, 92
 discovery of fraud, methods of, 106, 107
 importance of, 106
 internal audits, 110, 111
 key points, 105
 manual monitoring, 112
 as preventive measure, 92
 questions for assessing, 121
 responsibility for, 141
 skepticism, role of, 106
 technology-based, 112–117
 transaction monitoring, 106, 107
Deterrents
 code of ethics as deterrent to wrongdoing, 74
 and control environment, 67, 70, 88
 detective controls as, 10, 39, 92
 fraud avoidance and mitigation framework, 36
 hotline as, 78
 preventive controls as, 92
 technology, use of, 40
 testing of controls, 110
Dittmar, Lee, 85
Document retention practices, 133, 134
Double accounting systems, 54
Due diligence
 background checks as part of mergers and acquisitions, 95
 development of techniques for, 35
 hotlines, 78, 79

E

Economic downturns and risk of fraud, xxii, xxiii, 13, 152
Electronically stored information (ESI), 131–133

Email, 73, 78, 81, 99, 115,
130–133
Embezzlement, 128
Employees
background investigations,
80, 95
discipline, 81
hiring, 80
roles and responsibilities of in
risk management, 138, 142,
143, 148, 149
training in ethics and fraud
awareness, 15, 40, 41, 71,
77, 95
Enron, 16, 26
Enterprise risk management
(ERM)
basic concepts of, 82, 83
competitive benefits of, 84
described, 82
and preventive controls, 104
and risk intelligence, 83, 84
Epps, Donna, xvii
*Ethical Business Practice: Importance
for the Recruiting Process,* 97
Ethics
and background checks, 95
code of conduct for vendors,
business partners and agents,
99, 100
and corporate culture, 35
*Ethical Business Practice:
Importance for the Recruiting
Process,* 97
responsibility for, 38, 80
and tone at the top. *See* Tone at
the top
training, 77
Evaluation of preventive controls,
101
Evidence, 124, 130–133

Expectations, pressure to meet,
50–52, 94, 95, 98, 161, 162
External audits and auditors
control environment,
effectiveness of, 69
independent auditor
requirement, 144, 145

F
"Fears, Fires, Fleas and Flaws," 9,
61–64
Federal Communications
Commission, fraud
investigations, 27
Federal Rules of Civil Procedure,
131, 132
Federal Sentencing Guidelines,
80, 81
*Final Rule: Management's Reports on
Internal Control Over Financial
Reporting and Certification
of Disclosure in Exchange Act
Periodic Reports,* 141
Financial reporting, internal
controls over, 141, 145
Financial statement fraud
computerized tools for
detecting, 64
data interrogation techniques
for detecting, 115, 116
generally, 4
and level of perpetrators, 19
and manual monitoring, 112
preventive controls, 97, 98
and risk of management
override, 54, 55. *See also*
Management
SEC enforcement actions, 23, 24
Financial statements
financial reporting, internal
controls over, 141, 145

fraud. *See* Financial statement
fraud
management responsibilities,
140, 141
Fines and penalties, 26–28. *See also*
Criminal liability
Foreign Corrupt Practices Act
(FCPA)
compliance with and benefits of
risk management, 35
data interrogation techniques
for detecting violations of,
116, 117
increase in prosecutions, 7, 13,
47, 158
liability under, 26, 27
preventive controls, 100
Forensic accountants, 128
Framework for fraud avoidance
and mitigation, 34–36
Francis, Kerry, 127, 128
Fraud
consequences of, generally, 6
defined, 4
groups of fraud risks, 17
pervasiveness of, xv, xvi
and speed of evolution of fraud
risks, xxiii
Fraud avoidance and mitigation
framework, 34–36
Fraud control gap, xxiv
Fraud risk indicators, 51. *See also*
Risk factors
Fraud risk management
accountability for, 42
audit committee, role of, 39, 41,
52, 53, 68, 69, 136, 138, 139,
148
benefits of, xxv, xxvi, 35–37
board of directors, role of, 38,
39, 41, 138–140

and categories of risk, xxiii, xxiv
common areas for improvement, 40
and competitive advantage, 152
compliance officers, 147, 148
continuous improvement
approach (Measure, Improve,
and Move), 40, 41
and control environment, 69–71
as core competency, 17
cross-functional committee,
benefits of, 146, 147
dashboards, use of, 42
employees, roles and
responsibilities of, 138, 142,
143, 148, 149
gap analysis, 41, 42
internal audit, role of, 49, 69, 107,
136, 138, 141, 143, 144, 146
knowing your business,
importance of, 137
management, role of, 71, 125,
138, 140–142, 148
measuring performance, 154, 155
need for improvement, 14, 15
and periods of economic
turmoil, xxii, xxiii, 13, 152
principles of, 37, 38
proactive approach, xxiii, 37,
91–93, 145, 151, 152, 159
reactive approach, 37, 151, 153
roles and responsibilities, xxv,
136–146, 148, 149, 154, 157
scorecards, use of, 42
strategies for, 61–64, 71
support for, enlisting, 40, 41
and trends in fraud, 13, 14, 46
types of fraud most commonly
occurring in specific
industries, 18, 19
written policies, 71
Fraud schemes, identifying, 53–55

Fraudulent financial reporting. *See also* Financial statement fraud
 preventive controls, 97, 98
 risk factors for, 161–165
Fraudulent financial statements. *See* Financial statement fraud
Fujimoto, Gerry, 126, 127, 129
Future cost due to fraud, 22–23

G

Gap analysis, 41–42
Globalization
 bribery and corruption trends, xv
 and cultural differences, 5
 and risk of fraud, xxiii, 12, 13, 15, 16, 46, 47, 153, 155
Goldsmith, Barry, 125
Governance. *See also* Audit committee; Board of directors
 and benefits of risk management, 35
 changes since 2002, xvi, 136–146
 and control environment, responsibility for, 70
Governance, risk and compliance (GRC)
 characteristics of companies with integrated GRC, 87, 88
 complexity of, 85
 described, 84, 85
 integrated and non-integrated GRC compared, 85, 86
 integrated GRC as preference, 86, 87
 and preventive controls, 104
Guidance on Monitoring Internal Control Systems, 101, 103

H

Hartley, Bruce, 130
Hatton, Humphry, 25
Heat maps, use of, 8, 9, 60, 61

Hooker, Hugh, 37, 47
Hotlines. *See* Whistle-blower hotlines (helplines)
Human resources (HR)
 role of in investigation, 126
 as source of evidence, 130

I

Impact of fraud, limiting, 33
Incentives and pressures to perpetrate fraud
 asset misappropriation risk factors, 165
 excessive pressure to meet financial targets, 50–52, 94, 95, 98, 125
 fraudulent financial reporting, 161, 162
 as risk factor, 50–52, 94, 95
Independent auditors, 144, 145
Information technology (IT)
 automated controls, 80, 88, 96, 102, 112, 115, 124
 continuous fraud monitoring, 117–121
 and cross-functional risk management committee, 146
 and electronic evidence, 124, 130–133
 financial statement fraud, tools for detecting, 64
 and fraud deterrence, 40
 role of in anti-fraud programs, xxiv, xxv
 security and access controls, 99
Ingram, Gavin, xxii, 140
Instant messaging, 131, 132
Institute of Internal Auditors (IIA)
 International Standards for the Professional Practice of Internal Auditing, 111

Managing the Business Risk of Fraud: A Practical Guide, 38. *See also Managing the Business Risk of Fraud: A Practical Guide*
Internal audit
  audit committee oversight of, 70, 110, 143
  computer assisted techniques, 62
  and control environment, 73
  and cross-functional risk management committee, 146
  and financial controls design and effectiveness, 141
  fraud detected by, 106
  as fraud detection tactic, 110, 111
  Managing the Business Risk of Fraud: A Practical Guide. See Managing the Business Risk of Fraud: A Practical Guide
  monitoring activities, 101, 114
  preventive controls, role of in developing, 94, 135
  role of in fraud investigations, 126, 128, 129, 135
  role of in GRC policies and procedures, 88
  role of in risk assessment, 52, 53
  role of in risk management, 49, 69, 107, 136, 138, 141, 143, 144, 146
  testing of controls, 97, 98
  tone at the top, role of in setting, 73. *See also* Tone at the top
Internal controls. *See also* Detective controls; Preventive controls
  control environment. *See* Control environment
  entity level controls, 56
  and fraud risk factors, 52
  and fraud risks, misconceptions about, 94

and identifying possible risk, 53
  and internal audits, 110, 111
  management override of, 45, 50, 54, 55, 94, 97, 98, 101, 110, 139, 142, 143, 145
  mitigating impact of, evaluating, 56, 57
  over financial reporting, 141, 145
  process level controls, 56
  responsibility for, 141, 142
  and risk assessment, 46, 48
  strengthening as treatment for residual risk, 57, 58
  types of distinguished, 94
Internal Revenue Service, Criminal Investigations Division, 27
International Financial Reporting Standards (IFRS), transition to and risk of fraud, 156
Interviews as part of investigation, 132, 133
Investigations
  allegations, evaluating, 126, 127
  audit committee, role of, 125, 127, 128
  background investigations. *See* Background checks
  board of directors, role of, 123–128
  board oversight, 126
  case management systems, 124, 133, 134
  communication issues, 133
  complexity of, 123
  computer forensics, 124, 130, 131
  conducting, guidance for, 123, 124
  conducting, setting protocols for, 129, 130
  data, collecting and preserving, 130–133
  electronically stored information (ESI), 131–133

Investigations (*continued*)
evidence, 124, 130–133
external, 125, 126
fraud examination and
investigation, guidance for
anti-fraud measures, 34, 35
by government agencies, 27,
125, 126, 132
guidance for anti-fraud
measures, 34, 35
human resources, role of, 126
interviews, 124, 128, 129, 131
key points, 122
legal counsel, role of, 125–128, 134
legal standards for, 129–130
outside help, determining when
needed, 128, 129
planning, importance of,
124–126
and record keeping and
document retention practices,
123, 131, 132
remedial action, identifying,
126, 127, 134, 135
response plans, 124–126, 129
team, assembling, 127, 128

J

J-SOX, compliance with and benefits
of risk management, 35

K

Kammer, Christian, 13, 37
Key performance indicators
(KPIs), 155
Kickbacks, 115. *See also* Bribery and
corruption

L

Legal counsel
background investigation of, 80
communication, responsibility
for, 133
criminal liability, 26
and cross-functional risk
management committee, 146
and response plan, 126
role of in investigations, 125,
130, 133, 134
Likelihood of risk occurring, 55,
60, 61
Lilienfeld, Albert, 97
Listing standards
board of directors, role of in risk
management, 39
code of ethics requirements, 74
and corporate governance, 137,
138
Litigation. *See also* Criminal liability
class actions, 23
settlements, 23, 24
Lookbacks, 120, 121
Lucus, Paul, 115

M

Madoff, Bernard, xvi, 25
Management
background investigations, 80.
See also Background checks
code of ethics, monitoring of, 74
cooking the books, 52,
54–57, 63
ethics training for, 77
financial expectations, pressure
to meet, 50–52, 94, 95, 98,
161, 162
financial statements,
management responsibilities,
140, 141
investigation oversight, 125, 129
and listing standards, 138
override of internal controls, 45,
50, 54, 55, 94, 97, 98, 101, 110,
139, 142, 143, 145
preventive controls, 98
and response plan, 126

role of in risk assessment, 46, 50, 52, 53, 100

role of in risk management, 71, 138, 140–142, 148

Sarbanes-Oxley section 404, guidance for management, 141, 142

tone at the top, role of in setting, 71. *See also* Tone at the top

Management override of internal controls, 45, 50, 54, 55, 94, 97, 98, 101, 110, 139, 142, 143, 145

Managing the Business Risk of Fraud: A Practical Guide, 37–40, 42, 58, 92, 94, 123, 124, 138, 139, 148

McDermott, Elizabeth Truelove, xv

Measure, Improve, and Move methodology (continuous improvement), 40, 41

Media, 26, 159

Mergers and acquisitions, employee background checks, 80

Mexico
accounting practices, 54
and bribery, 48

Mitigation of risk
impact of internal controls. *See* Internal controls
management responsibilities, 140
and risk assessment, 48, 49

Money laundering
anti-money laundering software, xxiv
data interrogation techniques for detecting, 117

Monitoring
audit committee oversight of, 121
effectiveness of anti-fraud program, 154, 155

false positives, 17

manual monitoring, 112

preventive controls, 100–103

questions for assessing, 121

tools, 63

transaction monitoring, 106, 115

Moore's Law, 113

Multinational companies and impact of fraud, 15, 16

N

NASDAQ listing standards, 39, 74, 137, 138

New York Stock Exchange (NYSE) listing standards, 39, 74, 137, 138

Novosel, Mike, 73, 101, 102

O

Occupational Fraud and Abuse Classification System, 96, 97

Oil-for-Food Programme, 117, 144

Opportunity
as risk factor, 50, 51
risk factors for asset misappropriation, 166
risk factors for fraudulent financial reporting, 162–164

Organization for Economic Co-operation and Development (OECD), compliance with and benefits of risk management, 35

Organized crime, xxiii

P

Partnering Against Corruption Initiative (PACI), 88, 89

Pervasiveness of risk, assessing, 55

Phillipps, Tim, 15, 16

Pitt, Harvey, 137

Pollard, Bill, 123

Prevalence of fraud and
corruption, 3–5, 23
Prevention of fraud
common areas for improvement,
40
controls. *See* Preventive controls
as element of risk management,
5, 10
as first line of defense, 39
generally, 4
principles of risk management,
37, 38
Preventive controls
asset misappropriation, 98, 99
automated, 96. *See also*
Automation
background checks, 80, 95
bribery and corruption, 99, 100
and categories of risk, 96–100
continuous controls monitoring
(CCM), 102, 103
deficiencies, correcting, 103
described, 92
as deterrent to fraud, 92
and enterprise risk management
(ERM), 104
evaluation of, 101
fraudulent financial reporting,
97, 98
and governance, risk and
compliance (GRC) approach,
104
importance of, 92, 94, 95
key points, 91
management override of
internal controls, 97, 98, 101.
See also Management override
of internal controls
monitoring, 100–103
proactive approach, 91–93. *See
also* Proactive approach to risk
management

purpose of controls, 93
responsibility for, 141
and traditional approach to
fraud detection, 93
value of, 92
Proactive approach to risk
management, xxiii, 37, 91–93,
145, 151, 152, 159
Procurement fraud, data
interrogation techniques for
detecting, 114, 115
Public Company Accounting
Oversight Board (PCAOB),
Auditing Standard No. 5
control environment, 69
fraud controls, 97
independent auditor
requirement, 145
Public opinion, 26

Q

Quadrants of heat maps and risk
assessment, 8, 9, 61–64

R

Rationalization as risk factor, 50,
51, 164–167
Record keeping and document
retention practices,
133, 134
Regulatory compliance
and benefits of risk
management, 35
changes in regulations, 155
and compliance officers, 147,
148
as defense against fraud and
corruption, xvii
reporting fraud to agencies, 139
Remediation measures, 126, 127,
134, 135

Reports and reporting
  financial reporting, internal
    controls over, 141, 145
  financial reports, fraudulent. *See*
    Fraudulent financial reporting
  principles of risk management,
    38
  reporting fraud to regulatory
    agencies, 139
  risk assessment reports, 58–61
Reputational risk
  damage to reputation, 158
  due diligence, need for, 16
  and fraud, 37
  and increased public and
    regulatory scrutiny, 46
Residual risk, 56, 57
Resiliency
  as characteristic of successful
    companies, xviii
  characteristics of, 32, 33
  as corporate goal, 9–11
  and corporate policies, 33
  defined, 34, 160
  described, 32
  and risk management, 34
  self-assessment tool, 42–44
  traits of resilient corporation,
    32, 33
Response
  as element of fraud and
    corruption risk management,
    10, 11
  remediation measures as result
    of investigation, 126, 127,
    134, 135
Response plan, 124–126
Return on investment (ROI), 63
Rial, Ed, 16
Risk assessment
  audit committee, role of, 52–54
  board of directors, role of, 139

common areas for improvement,
  48, 50
corporate resiliency self-
  assessment tool, 42–44
by country, 48
described, 46
and effectiveness of policies,
  45, 56
as element of fraud and
  corruption risk management, 10
framework for, 58, 59
frequency of, 47
heat maps, use of, 8, 9, 60, 61
of identified risks, 55
importance of, 47–50, 153, 154
and internal controls, 48
internal controls, evaluating
  mitigating impact of, 56, 57
likelihood of risk occurring, 55
management, role of, 46, 50, 52,
  53, 100
and management override
  of internal controls. *See*
  Management
opportunities for improvement,
  64, 65
pervasiveness of risk, 55
possible risks, schemes and
  accounts affected, identifying,
  53–55
principles of risk management,
  38
prioritizing risks, 48, 55
process for, overview, 49
process for, steps for
  implementing, 50–58
purpose of, 48
quadrants, 8, 9, 61–64
reports, 58–61
residual risks, prioritizing for
  treatment, 57
responsibility for, 52

Risk assessment (*continued*)
  results, evaluating, 57
  risk factors, identifying, 50–53
  significance of risk, 55
Risk factors
  asset misappropriation,
    165–167
  categories of, 51
  evaluating, 52
  excessive pressure to meet
    financial targets, 50–52, 94,
    95, 98, 161, 162
  fraudulent financial reporting,
    161–165
  identifying and evaluating,
    50–53
  list of, 51, 161
  methods for identifying, 52, 53
Risk intelligence, 83, 84, 104
Risk management. *See* Fraud risk
    management
Risk tolerance, 48, 49, 56, 57, 63
Rosenberg, Ed, 7

S

Sarbanes-Oxley Act
  anti-fraud controls,
    responsibility for, 141–142
  board of directors, oversight role
    in risk management, 39
  code of ethics requirement, 74
  compliance audits,
    incorporating monitoring
    into, 102
  compliance with and benefits of
    risk management, 35
  guidance to management, 141,
    142
  impact of, 136, 137
  internal control over financial
    reporting, 141, 145

likelihood of risk occurring,
    assessing, 55
  section 404 guidance for
    management, 141, 142
  significance of risk, assessing, 55
  whistle-blower and hotline
    requirements, 78, 79. *See
    also* Whistle-blower hotlines
    (helplines)
Schirber, Mary Jane, 5
Schmidt, Wendy, 95, 96
Scorecards, use of, 42
Securities and Exchange
    Commission (SEC)
  Accounting and Auditing
    Enforcement Releases
    (AAERs), 23
  enforcement actions for
    financial statement fraud, 23,
    24
  *Final Rule: Management's
    Reports on Internal Control
    Over Financial Reporting and
    Certification of Disclosure in
    Exchange Act Periodic Reports,*
    141
  fraud investigations, 27
  Guidance to Management
    (Release 33-8810), 46
  and stock exchange listing
    standards, 137. *See also* Listing
    standards
Self-assessment of corporate
    resiliency, 42–44
Separation of duties, 18
Significance of risk
  assessing, 55
  heat maps, use of, 8, 9, 60, 61
Silos and use of cross-functional
    risk management committee,
    146, 147

Staff. *See* Employees

Standard and Poor's (S&P), risk management evaluation, 14, 25

Statement on Auditing Standards SAS No. 1, *Codification of Auditing Standards and Procedures,* 144

Statistics on costs of fraud. *See* Costs of fraud and corruption

Strategy
anti-fraud tactics versus anti-fraud strategies, 5, 6
fraud risk management strategies, 61–64, 71

Structuring transactions, 117

Survivability, 31, 32

Swinehart, Greg, 155

T

Technology and risk of fraud, xxiii, xxiv, xxv, 156. *See also* Information technology (IT)

Thomas, Duleep, 4

Tips, role of in uncovering fraud. *See* Whistle-blower hotlines (helplines)

Tone at the top, 68, 69, 71–74, 139–141, 143, 147, 157, 158, 160

Trade secrets, 99

Training in ethics and fraud awareness, 15, 40, 41, 71, 77, 95

Transparency
emphasis on, 16
and past experiences with fraud, xvii, 17

Transparency International, 88, 153

Trends impacting fraud risk, 12–15, 46, 155, 156

2008 Report to the Nation on Occupational Fraud and Abuse, 19, 21, 22, 78, 93, 96, 106, 107

Types of fraud, 4, 18

U

Ugeh, Patrick, 88

U.S. Patriot Act, compliance with and benefits of risk management, 35

U.S. Postal Inspection Service, fraud investigations, 27

U.S. sentencing guidelines
compliance with, 35
and management responsibilities, 80, 81

V

Villalobos, Jorge Garcia, 54

Vincze, Steve, 147, 148

Volcker, Paul, 144

Vulnerability, reducing, 32, 33

W

Web sites
Deloitte Forensic Center (DFC), 156
hotline reporting mechanisms, 78, 109
and rapid spread of news, 25

Weisman, Adam, 17, 94

Whistle-blower hotlines (helplines)
allegations, evaluating, 126, 127
attitudes toward, 79, 107
and case management systems, 134
characteristics of good programs, 79, 80
and duration of fraud, 93
as fraud deterrent, 78

Whistle-blower hotlines (helplines)
(*continued*)
and losses due to fraud, 93
management override,
preventing, 101
oversight by board and audit
committee, 139
performance improvement,
108–110
requirement for, xvi

tips, detection of fraud through,
78, 106, 143
use of, obstacles to, xvi, xvii
Williams, David, 79
World Economic Forum,
Partnering Against
Corruption Initiative (PACI),
88, 89
WorldCom, 16
Written code, 74–77

Printed in the United States
By Bookmasters